HOW TO
MAKE
$1000
GROW

BY HERBERT DALMAS

How To Make $1000 Grow

Fowler Formula

Exit Screaming

HOW TO MAKE $1000 GROW

HERBERT DALMAS

DOUBLEDAY & COMPANY, INC., GARDEN CITY, NEW YORK
1973

ISBN: 0-385-05767-9
Library of Congress Catalog Card Number 72–83138
Copyright © 1973 by Herbert Dalmas and Elizabeth Dalmas
All Rights Reserved
PRINTED IN THE UNITED STATES OF AMERICA
First Edition

To Paul Reynolds

CONTENTS

PREFACE

Elizabeth Dalmas worked with me on this book. There must be others who can match her wisdom, her patience, or her skill; but I doubt that there exists her equal in all three.

I am grateful for advice from:
Lerie Bjornstedt, of Ojai Realty, on real estate in general,
William Redding, of Blyth & Co., on real estate investment trusts,
Jerome T. Oss, of Paine, Webber, Jackson & Curtis, on rules and current practices of the New York and American Stock Exchanges,
Rubin & Taylor, commodity brokers, members of the Winnipeg Grain Exchange, on how United States citizens can trade on that exchange,
T. Horne, manager of the Commodity Department, Richardson Securities of Canada, on procedures of the Winnipeg Exchange, and
Robert L. Bevier, of Reynolds Securities, on commodity trading in general.
I am also grateful to John Lombardo, of Reynolds Securities, who was kind enough to read the manuscript from the technical point of view.

1

A thousand dollars can be important money

Money was invented to be used—bury it or keep it hidden in a vault and it might as well not exist. So much of it is being used around the world these days that you don't expect to see $1000 in the headlines very often, but the things it will buy are still beyond counting—and you can still make money with it. As a matter of fact, although this isn't publicized much, you can sometimes make quite a lot.

The $1000 we will be talking about in these pages is $1000 *outside* your budget. Maybe you saved it or it was willed to you, or maybe it was a present or a bonus—no matter: it isn't earmarked for something already planned for you or for anybody you are responsible for. You can do what you please with it and you won't risk missing a mortgage payment or an insurance premium or having to curtail your child's education plans. It is totally uninhibited money. You might want to put it away in a bank or buy a few shares of a blue chip stock. Maybe you'll feel like taking a few chances with it, and if you do, there's nothing to stop you. In the financial world, of course, you don't take chances; you assume risk.

The most important thing to keep in mind about risk is that you can't avoid it. Some things you do involve more of it than others, but nothing is completely without it: you don't ordinarily think of staying at home as being risky, but one of our best-known statistics shows that more accidents happen at home than anywhere else. About the best you can hope to do is see a risk in advance and act accordingly, but there will always be something you can't control. Modern air travel is as safe as any other kind, but think of the people buying plane tickets who wouldn't want to give you odds that they won't end up in Cuba.

Success in handling money depends on being able

1. to see all the risks possible to see in any situation;

2. to understand those that can be measured and how to measure them and to recognize those that can't be measured at all; and

3. to understand how much risk you are willing to take and how you will react and respond when something happens you couldn't possibly have foreseen but which may seem to threaten your project with disaster.

This book is a guide to 1 and 2. 3 is just as important, but nobody can do anything about it but yourself. If you go into a venture and someone with a lot of experience tells you it is rank speculation, that could be disquieting—but not if you have thought about it and decided you *want* to speculate. You will hear phrases like "intelligent investor" and that sounds like something you ought to want to be. But investing and speculating are only two ends of the same scale of risk, and the people operating at one end are just as smart and respectable as the people at the other. The thing to guard against is speculating in something like soybean futures if your emotions and nerves need the kind of stability you find in AT&T. And don't even get into AT&T if a price drop is going to make you worry about whether your money is safe.

The trick is to be as certain as you can be about yourself, to have some idea in advance how you will behave in any foreseeable situation, and to be confident that you won't disappoint yourself in the crises that come out of nowhere. It may sound easy. Just remember it isn't.

There are people who would prefer to reduce the risks with their money to a minimum, and they will find as close to absolute safety as exists anywhere in a savings account. As this is being written, banks and savings associations are offering the highest interest rates they have paid in recent history and telling the world about the thousands of satisfied people who are entrusting their money to them. They offer such lures as insurance on accounts up to $20,000, free notary service, and lounges with complimentary coffee; for large accounts there are free safety deposit boxes and free travelers' checks. The interest on savings varies with the amount on deposit and the length of time you agree to leave it there. At the present time, the range is from 5% to 6%.

Banks and savings associations guarantee that you will get back what you deposit with them, but they don't mention the risk you are assuming—possibly because it has been around so long that we have just about come to accept it as part of our way of life. The risk is that if you leave your money in the account for a year or so it won't buy as much when you take it out as it would have bought when you deposited it—even with the interest added. The name for this is inflation.

There is always talk about doing something to stop inflation, but most of us don't honestly expect it to disappear. Things at the market cost one or two cents apiece more than they did a couple of weeks ago. . . . So? Maybe things will slow down and the next raise won't come for a month. Cigarettes go up two cents a pack; gas is three cents more a gallon—it's only pennies, pinpricks. But we're even hardened to the jolts: announcements out of Detroit that next year's models are going to cost a hundred dollars more than this year's just barely catch our attention.

Anyone who spends money and thinks finds it hard to believe that $1050, which is what you would have in a savings account this time next year if you put $1000 in today, will buy as much as the $1000 will right now. Clearly, the solution to your personal problems of inflation is more money. One of the most effective ways of producing more money that anyone has discovered so far is by using money itself. People who urge you to join in this activity call it putting your money to work. Those already busy at it call it investing or speculating. However you think of it, there are many forms—but they all fall into either of two categories: lending or buying.

You lend your money when you put it into a savings account. The interest you get is rent—money for permission to use your money to make money. The bank lends your money to other people, sometimes people like yourself who want to buy cars or fix up their homes. Often they lend it to the government or private corporations. A lot of it goes into real estate. It is possible at times for you to lend your money on real estate too.

If you want to buy something with interesting possibilities for profit, the best fields are real estate and the stock market.

There are situations in either lending or buying when, just because of the nature of the situation itself, money's money-making power is greatly increased. When you choose one of these, you are "leveraging." Wall Street invented the verb, but human beings have used leverage since one of our prehistoric ancestors found he could throw a rock farther and harder with a sling than he could with his unaided arm. Leverage is a means of converting a comparatively small force into a much greater one. You can see a vivid example of it when there is a tire to be changed. Grab the bumper of the car and do your best to lift the wheel off the ground. You can't do it. With leverage, though—in this case provided by a jack—you can do it with one hand.

When a bank or savings association offers you a sum equal to 5% of your $1000 for permission to use it, leverage becomes possible. The $50 the bank pays you brings into action the power of $1000, just as your one hand brings into action the power of the jack. By lending your $1000 at interest rates from 7¼% to 18%, the bank makes a profit on its $50 of from $25 to $130. If it had been able to lend only the $50 at the same rates, the profits would have been just $3.63 to $9.00.

You can leverage your $1000. Of course banks use other ways to make money with money—and you can use them too. What method you decide on depends on your temperament and how much time and thought and energy you can afford to spend. But you've got more options than a bank has. The law requires organizations investing other people's money to be ultraconservative. With your uninhibited $1000, you can go into moneymaking areas not open to even some of the most powerful financial giants.

REAL ESTATE

How to be a
landlord on $1000

Everyone knows what mortgages are, but most people learn the details when they get a loan from a bank to buy a house they expect to live in. Naturally, when you do that, you pay as much as you can to start so the balance will be as small as possible and the monthly payments easier. You aren't concerned with leverage. It's different when you buy a house as a way of making money. That is income property, and your profit depends on how much you have to spend. You want to spend what is necessary to get the property and to improve it—but not more than is necessary, so when you arrange financing you want to make the smallest down payment permissible. This will mean larger monthly payments, but with income property they should be covered by what the tenant pays you. Ultimately, you expect to sell the house for a capital gain. This is a simple form of leverage used by practically everybody who buys real estate to make money.

The "real" in "real estate," incidentally, isn't the opposite of "unreal." It is a French word meaning "royal" and is a relic of the days when all land belonged to the king or queen. "Estate" comes from a word which meant "to stand," so originally real estate was evidence of where the monarch "stood" with regard to property.

Today, there are two kinds of real estate: unimproved land and land with something on it—a building or some kind of crop. Ordinarily, a bank or savings association prefers not to lend money on unimproved land. This is because if it should be necessary to foreclose the mortgage and take possession of the property, taxes on it would have to be paid, and the bank doesn't want to risk having to pay them with nothing coming in. Selling the land could take time, and selling land isn't a bank's business.

Improved land is just the opposite—it can pay its own way: a building can be rented or a crop sold for enough to cover mortgage payments, insurance, and taxes—and usually for something more.

If you have a chance to buy a piece of unimproved land for enough under your $1000 to be sure you have enough left over to pay the taxes until the land increases in value, and if you are certain the price *will* go up, and if you know beyond doubt that this will happen before you run out of money —buy it. Otherwise, stay with income property.

The best you can do for $1000 is a house you can buy for not more than $15,000. You probably won't find anything at all in the center of a large city, but in small towns or the edges of big-city suburbs there are often houses in the two-bedroom, one-bath category for that price. Outside metropolitan areas, you will often find the same houses for less than $15,000. In those places, your $1000 can be leveraged into something even larger. You will find that no two situations will be exactly alike, even in the same community.

The price being asked for the house won't necessarily be what you'll end up paying. As often as not, real estate sales are negotiated. People will pay according to how badly they want to live in the place or how much money they think they can make from it. People sell to get money, and what they will take depends on why and how soon they want it.

An example is the true story of Mrs. King, a widow living in a small western New York State town. She owned her house outright, and she had a comfortable income.

One day she heard by chance that two small houses on the same parcel of land in town were about to be offered for sale. She knew the owner only by name, but she also knew the houses had never been vacant for more than a month and only once or twice that she could remember, so he must have been making money. Why did he want to sell? She went to see him and asked.

It turned out he was in a great hurry. He had a chance to make a lot of money in another part of the country, but to do it he had to raise $15,000 right away. He was willing to sell the two houses for $20,000, which was the price his bank had appraised them at.

Mrs. King was smart enough not to try to bargain; the owner was clearly interested in getting cash in a hurry and was offering a quick-sale price. On the other hand, the most the bank would lend was $16,000, and that left $4000 for her to pay. She could have raised it easily by mortgaging her own house, but she was thrifty and she hadn't had any experience in this kind of thing, so she hesitated.

The owner didn't want to wait. He offered to take a second mortgage for $3000. Surely Mrs. King could scrape up $1000.

She could do that all right. The owner went over the figures with her and showed that the rents from the houses would more than cover her running expenses. Getting $1000 on her house was no problem. The bank holding the first mortgage on the houses she was buying would have preferred her to have at least a 10% equity in them, which would have meant a down payment of $2000, but the owner had been a customer there for a long time, and he persuaded them to make an exception. An added inducement was Mrs. King's excellent credit rating.

As the new owner, Mrs. King raised the rents only once—and that wasn't until two years later, after she had made some improvements. The income gave her a nice return on her investment every year for seven years.

Recently she had an offer of $28,000 for the property. By now she had other real estate ideas—and she closed for $28,500.

Mrs. King's experience isn't unique, but she was lucky because no great effort was required of her. Normally, you have to work harder than that for your profits. Like Mr. West, who lives on the other side of the continent.

In July 1971, Mr. West heard of a property in the town where he lives that was being offered for sale at $10,000. He thought the house had possibilities, but it needed work; it was work Mr. West would be able to do himself, but it would mean giving up a few weekends and he couldn't see himself doing that without the prospect of a worthwhile profit. He offered $6000.

He was surprised when the offer was accepted. It turned out the owner was selling because he wanted very much to move east. He still owed $3000 on the house, and $6000 would give him $3000 cash and a loss that would lower his income tax.

Mr. West paid 10% down—$600—and his bank loaned him $5400. He spent five weekends spread over two months and a half getting the house the way he wanted it, and when he had finished, it looked like new. He didn't have any trouble finding a tenant at $115 a month.

At the end of his first year of owning the property, Mr. West's income will be only $1035, because he will have got only nine months' rent. But when he fills out his income tax form, he will be able to take a deduction equal to the property tax, plus the interest on the mortgage, plus a depreciation allowance (which we will explain later), plus the cost of the improvements he made. Of course, he didn't pay himself in cash, but he is entitled to a fair return for his labor, and when all the arithmetic has been done, he will find that his deductions for income tax purposes will be about $500 more than what he gets from the house. Furthermore, the property is in so much better shape than it was that the bank will take a mortgage for a higher amount than it did the first time. The new payments will be larger, but they will be covered by the rent. After refinancing expenses and paying off the original loan, Mr. West figures to clear more than $2000. This money is tax free.

There are three points to be made from these experiences. First, moneymaking properties do exist that, using the leveraging process, you can gain title to with your $1000. Second, if you keep up a rentable property, as Mrs. King kept up hers, it will increase in value. Third, you can accelerate that increase by making judicious improvements.

The first requirements of the house you will be looking for are that it will be in a well-cared-for neighborhood and that you will be able to improve it. Since the improvements that have the best financial effect are ones you can see, your best bet will be a place that looks a bit run down compared with those around it. Faded, even slightly peeling paint or grounds that have become a little ragged will be attractive from your point of view, because they give you a chance to accomplish so much for so little. (If you don't happen to have talents like Mr. West's, you may have to spend some money, and your $1000 is already committed to the down payment. This can be handled; we'll come to it in a moment.)

While you are in the looking-around stage, you may come across a commercial property that seems tempting. It won't be an office building at $15,000, but it could be a store. No matter how persuasive a sales pitch you get from the owner, proceed with caution. Such properties are more complicated to manage than houses are. Also, unless the location is ideal, you will be assuming quite a risk, which will be about the same whether the business renting from you succeeds or fails. Success would be motivation to move to a better location—and if a business fails, it just moves out. Either way, you have an empty store on your hand, and vacant stores seem to stay that way longer than houses do.

Let's say you've seen a house you think has possibilities, and you find that the owner is represented by a real estate broker we'll call Mrs. Sage. You will assume Mrs. Sage's honesty; what is important to you is how much she knows about real estate. A good way to get a line on this is to go to the bank nearest her office and ask the manager if he can recommend three or four real estate brokers he would consider competent to handle the sale of a residential property for someone who has very little experience in such matters. It won't hurt to let him think the person you are talking about is yourself.

He will probably mention Mrs. Sage. If he doesn't, start looking again.

Books have been written about how to choose income property and how to protect yourself against some of the innumerable hazards the non-professional is bound to find in his path. It would be a good idea to have such a book handy for reference; however, to try, before you start on a project, to absorb everything it has to say might very well mean that you wouldn't get started for a long time, if at all. The purpose here is to tell you some of the important things you can and should do. The reference books are also valuable for pointing out the things you should *not* do. In that category, there is room here for just one rule, and you should never in any circumstances break it. Be sure you read and understand every word of anything you have to sign, even if you feel a little silly insisting on it. You may have to take a document home with you, but a few extra hours can't spoil the deal and they could easily keep you from making a costly mistake. Whatever you don't understand ask to have explained and if necessary have the explanation repeated until you are satisfied that you are clear on every detail.

Before you make an offer for the property you are thinking about, there are several things to check on. You will want to know if it has changed hands during the past few years and, if so, how often. If this has happened several times, each at a higher price, the profit limit may have been reached—at least temporarily.

If the house is vacant, find out why. Repeated turnover of tenants during its rental life is a bad sign; maybe it was the landlord's fault and you might do better, but if the reason has something to do with the house itself, it could be something you wouldn't have the money to fix.

Think about location. The house will be easier to rent if it is on a street where there is no heavy or fast traffic, and if it is a convenient distance from markets, schools, churches, and public transportation. The last is particularly important for a one-car family. In communities where the residential and business sections are still separated, you should have a fairly accurate idea of how long they will stay that way. When the first store appears in a neighborhood, the location's desirability as a place to live starts to go down.

Inside the house, look for stains on the upstairs ceiling or on any of the walls. If you see any, stop thinking about the house then and there. They mean leaks, and fixing leaks means more money than you have available for this project.

People who want to rent a house, if they are satisfied with the location, think next about the size and arrangement of rooms and whether or not there is adequate closet space. A bedroom should be able to hold a bed, a chest of drawers, at least one comfortable chair, and a bedside table without the person using it feeling cramped. The living room should be large enough so that four people can sit and talk comfortably as long as they want to. It helps to have a place for the television set other than the living room, but that isn't always possible. Informal eating arrangements are all right for the family at breakfast and lunch, but there ought to be a place where people at the dinner table don't have to look into the kitchen.

There should be a closet for each bedroom, one for linens, one in the kitchen, and a utility closet near the front door. If you have ever done much in a kitchen, you know how important the cupboards and cabinets are. If this is unfamiliar territory to you, ask a knowledgeable friend to come along and give an opinion. Probably as many houses have been rejected by prospective renters because of an inadequate kitchen as for any other single reason.

Kitchen and bathroom floors are important. Cracked or chipped linoleum or tile might be easy and cheap to fix—or not. Find out exact costs for this, because even if a family moves into the house without mentioning it, sooner or later they will be after you to set it right.

People like electric fixtures that are good-looking and, above all, firm. A sagging wall light not only looks bad, it is probably dangerous. And there ought to be plenty of places to plug in appliances convenient to where they are going to be used. Including the bathroom.

Outside again, look at the roof gutters and downspouts. If they are loose or worn through, they could cost somebody a lot of money, and you don't want it to be you. However, if you didn't see water stains inside the house, they aren't responsible for damage yet and replacing them is the kind of improvement that can boost the value of a house for relatively little cost.

Then there is the garage. It should have a solid floor and watertight walls and roof. It's an even bet that this one has these, and the evidence is that if the house has been occupied for a year or so the garage has become the family repository for everything not in use at the moment—except the car. This is because storage space is lacking inside the house, which is too bad, because there ought to be room to keep a car, not only out of the weather but out of sight. When a car stands in the driveway all the time and then disappears for a few days, it doesn't take much reasoning to figure the family is away. This fact is of great interest to vandals and burglars.

The point of mentioning this is that it wouldn't cost much to have an addition put onto the service porch. This would provide storage space and is another thing that would add quite a bit to the value of the house.

You will have been uncomfortably aware how often some improvement has been mentioned, always with the assurance that it won't cost much. That's fine till you add them up—and anyway all of your $1000 is going for the down payment, so even one item is out of the question.

Well, you don't have to make the improvements right now. Tenants always expect a new landlord to raise the rent, but your only justification for doing that would be improvements, and if you postpone them the rent stays the same and the tenants are surprised—and happy. You can do the work as you go along and pay for it out of the difference between the income from rent and your fixed expenses: mortgage payments, taxes, and insurance. This difference, on a $15,000 house, will be

[16]

around $300 a year anywhere: while rents and taxes vary from locality to locality, they always do so in pretty much the same relationship; $300 a year is a return of 30% on your $1000.

This $300 is taxable, but since your property brings you income, you may take deductions which will more than cancel it as far as income tax is concerned. You are permitted deductions for mortgage interest and property taxes on any real property, but with income property there is, in addition, a depreciation allowance.

The law gives you this because it recognizes the fact that anything you use to make money will wear out sometime and have to be replaced; it says you may put aside each year enough money to buy a new whatever-it-is when the one you are using has come to the end of its useful life, and this sum may be deducted from income for tax purposes. The IRS doesn't insist that you actually establish such a fund; you may take the deduction anyway.

If you have a twenty-five-year mortgage on your income property, the useful life of the property is presumed to be twenty-five years and it may be "depreciated," as the accountants say, at the rate of 4% a year. As 4% of $15,000 is $600, you may add that sum to your deductions. You will find that the total is then slightly more than the income you get from the property, so that the actual $300 is free and clear.

But what about those improvements? Part, or maybe even all, of the first year's $300 ought to go for this purpose. It isn't likely that you would have bought a property that needed all the improvements we have mentioned; any one of them will contribute to enhancing its value.

Again, the cost of such work will vary with the locality, and it goes without saying that you shouldn't contract for a job at the first price quoted to you unless you are certain it is the best you can get. You have to shop around to find good work done reasonably, and if you are a novice at that sort of thing, be patient. You're not going to start the work until some money has come in anyway, so you will have time to talk to people who have had experience. At income tax time, of course, you can add the cost of the improvement to your other deductions. And the improvement will justify raising the rent.

All this is on the assumption that you have bought the house. However, after you have decided you want it, several things have to happen before it becomes yours.

First, you have to be sure a bank will take a mortgage for enough to put it within reach of your $1000. We are assuming the bank appraises the property at $15,000. It will lend you 80% of that: $12,000. This is $3000 short of the purchase price, so now you need someone who will take a second mortgage for $2000. As a rule, banks won't take second mortgages, but often the seller is glad to and sometimes even the real estate broker will do it. Second mortgages run from five to seven years with a maximum interest rate of 10%.

When you are ready to make your offer, Mrs. Sage will draw up a purchase contract that will put in writing what you agree to do and what the seller agrees to do and the time limits within which you each agree to do it. Mrs. Sage will be acting for the seller; you are the only one who will be thinking primarily of *your* interests, and you ought to be immovable where they are concerned. Remember the rule about understanding every word of the contract before you sign it. It would be a good idea to get Mrs. Sage to give you a rough draft, then show it to a lawyer or a friend who has had real estate experience. If changes, deletions, or additions should be made in your interest, insist on them. There is no reason to believe that Mrs. Sage or the seller is out to cheat you, but anybody can forget a point—and taking something for granted that doesn't happen could bind you to something you don't want to be bound to. For example, Mrs. Sage might tell you there will be no trouble at all getting the loans you want. She will truly believe this and so will you, but suppose the bank has some ideas you don't know about yet or the second mortgagee has second thoughts? Have it stated clearly that, if either loan is denied or the conditions changed in any detail from the way you want it, there is no sale.

When a buyer signs one of these agreements, it is customary to pay a deposit—from 5% to 10% of the purchase price. It is

[18]

the broker's responsibility to get as large a deposit as possible; but this is sometimes called "earnest money" because it shows that the buyer is serious about the offer, and you can be just as serious with $750, which is 5% of the purchase price, as you could be with your entire $1000. There is no reason for Mrs. Sage not to accept it, and it is sound policy never to part with more cash than you have to.

Have it stipulated clearly in the contract that if the sale falls through your deposit will be returned in full. Have it stipulated also that if your offer is not accepted within ten days— or less time if you think it best—the whole deal is off, and your deposit will be returned in full. Never forget to add that phrase "in full." Unless you insist on this time limit, the seller can use your offer to prod other prospective buyers into action at higher prices.

Finally, be sure the property is clearly and completely described in the contract.

At this point, some states require a period called "escrow" during which everything is in abeyance while the title is searched and the buyer arranges the details of financing. The cost of this is usually around $100, and the buyer and seller each pays half. In states not having the escrow requirement, it is practically always the seller who pays for the title search.

If the seller tells you a search is not necessary because one was made two months ago—or last week—and the title was perfectly clear, he may not just be trying to save money, he may really believe it. But insist on the search anyhow. Strange, sometimes apparently impossible things can happen. Recently, a California landlord put down wall-to-wall carpeting in a house and sold it shortly afterward. Through a human error, the money he paid for the carpeting was credited to a wrong account. The landlord, of course, was not aware of this; he didn't think a title search was necessary and none was made. The result was that not long after the new owner took possession the company that had put down the carpeting put a lien on the house to recover its money. The fact that the landlord had paid didn't make any difference; there was no record of the fact where it should have been, and in a situation like that the claim is against the property, not the individual. So the new owner was actually not the owner at all because the title was clouded, and there was a legal snarl costing time and money that wouldn't have had to be spent if the title had been properly searched.

Earlier we mentioned that Mr. West refinanced the house he had bought and refurbished and had cleared more than $2000, which was tax free. Refinancing simply means changing the existing mortgage on the property for a new one. If the new one is for a larger sum the difference is yours in cash. In the situation we have just been describing, it would work this way.

Real property, if it is well kept up and if the neighborhood it is in is also well maintained, will increase in value as a matter of course. The rate of increase is generally estimated at about 3% a year. Any improvements will accelerate this a bit, but we will figure conservatively and say that after five years, the house you have just bought should be appraised by a lending institution at $17,000.

Now you can get another loan, this time for 80% of $17,000, which is $13,600. Your original loan was for $12,000, and after five years there will be $10,980 left to pay on it. Added to this will be refinancing charges, but they won't come to more than $500. The total, subtracted from the $13,600, will leave you more than $1000 in cash.

This $1000-plus is a loan and you don't have to pay an income tax on it: loans aren't income, because they have to be paid back. This one is paid back, just as the original one on the property was, in monthly payments; but when you are making payments on a rental property, they don't come out of your pocket: they come out of the rent your tenants pay you, and you should be sure the rent is high enough to cover them. However, since higher mortgage payments will reduce your profit from the rent, you should generally refinance only to raise cash for investment, or soon before you sell the property, provided you know you won't have to pay too much in pre-payment penalties (see next paragraph).

In applying for a loan at any time, when you buy property or refinance, you should keep in mind that interest rates change, and it is clearly to your advantage to assume a mortgage when those rates are down rather than up. Remember also that banks differ from one another in their lending procedures and that savings and loan associations differ as a class from banks. A savings and loan, for example, will sometimes lend more than 80% on a property, a bank almost never. On the other hand, when you change from one mortgage to another, a savings association will very likely charge you a prepayment fee, which is usually about six months' interest on the original mortgage. This is a penalty for paying off the mortgage before it has run its full course. Some banks will do this, but many won't. Before you assume responsibility for any mortgage, you should shop around for the best terms.

Your first income property should return your $1000 and something more. In time, you may want to sell it, but the profit you make will be taxed as capital gain, so be sure it is large enough to make it worth while to give up the income.

Remember that what is set down in these pages is intended as a guide and, like any guide, can only point the way. It can tell you some of the things to do and to look out for, but you should always be prepared to be confronted with details you may not even have known the existence of before. Real estate laws differ from state to state, and they are intricate and complicated everywhere; sometimes procedures differ within a state. And there is always your own individual tax situation, which will have a vital bearing on every money decision you make.

Almost always a competent real estate broker will be able to give you the information you need. It is worth your while to form a working relationship with such a professional: when you are the buyer, of course, you will know that he or she is primarily representing the interests of the seller; but most brokers are interested in seeing that both parties to a deal get fair treatment—and, besides, ultimately you expect to be a seller yourself.

If your temperament is such that, particularly if you haven't had experience, you'd feel better if you didn't go alone into a project like the one we've been describing, you could do

HOW TO MAKE $1000 GROW

the same thing with a small syndicate. This would also broaden your range of opportunity.

A syndicate is simply a group of people who get together to make money from money. There have been real estate syndicates in this country since the middle of the last century; some have been very large, some have had only a few members, but one thing those you will have heard about have in common is that each member has put up a lot more than $1000. This is because syndicates are usually formed to buy properties often priced in the millions of dollars and to provide tax benefits attractive to people in the high brackets. But a small syndicate with each person putting in $1000 is feasible, and it could be profitable. With five members, the pooled money could leverage a property appraised up to $40,000.

No syndicate just happens: somebody has to get it together, and that person has to have something to motivate the group. Let's say, in the syndicate we are going to talk about, the person is you.

You should start by having in mind a definite property you know can be bought. You should research it so you'll be able to answer the questions anyone might ask who would be interested in buying it. Who is the owner and why does he want to sell? What opportunities are there for improvement that will make it worth more money? How much will the improvements cost—approximately? What income does the property bring now and are there possibilities of increasing it? What price is the owner asking; is there any reason to think he would take less? Is he still paying on a mortgage? He probably is, so what bank holds it and what would the bank assess the property at now? What are taxes and insurance?

When you have this information, you will be able to decide whether it would be a good buy. If it is, you can demonstrate to four other people how it would be profitable.

A membership of five is not a random suggestion. More than that would be unwieldy when decisions have to be made; fewer might not give you the healthiest possible range of opinion and might result in one strong personality dominating the others. All five should be people who already know one another and get along well together.

If you have done all the preliminary work just outlined, you might feel you deserve a little something more than the others—a small fee, perhaps, or maybe you should be the syndicate manager. You will form your syndicate faster and things will run more smoothly afterward if you resist this temptation. Other people, especially your friends, will be more inclined to go along with you if they feel your personal contribution and profit are exactly what theirs will be, and if you have already made an extra effort, they will be more willing to offer an equivalent when it is needed.

All formal syndicates have managers, but the one we are talking about here should not. Problems should be discussed by all the members, and the decisions should be unanimous. One or more of the members may have specialized knowledge or experience that is valuable to the project, but this should not be translated into added authority or even responsibility.

However, the syndicate will need professional help, and the reference books already mentioned won't quite do it. The members ought to have easy access to such books, but real estate may not be the profession of any of you, and the syndicate needs the advice and help of someone who is familiar with real estate law in the state where you are operating and who has contacts with banks and other professionals. This person will be a competent real estate broker with experience in the kind of property you are considering.

All you need to hold the syndicate together is a written document. It doesn't have to be anything formal, like a limited partnership, for example, which many syndicates are; it is enough for the members to agree on what they will contribute and how they will share.

First, the agreement should describe the property the syndicate is going to buy. It should state that each member is contributing $1000 and that there will be no further assessments.

This is different from the practice of most small syndicates. Usually, the members agree to share expenses equally, but we are talking about what *you* can do with $1000, and your fellow members shouldn't have to spend more even if they could do it easily.

Therefore, since there may always be unexpected needs for cash, the syndicate should consider only property that can be bought with $4000 down. With $5000 in the pool, the syndicate will thus have $1000 for contingencies. It isn't likely that you will use anywhere near all the reserve, but just having it there will give everybody a sense of security. None of it should be spent unless there is no other way. If you have to go into it for things like a consulting fee for your real estate broker or liability insurance, the money should be put back out of income.

The agreement should say further that equity in the property will be shared equally by the members, that they will share equally in the net income from the property and in any net capital gain from its sale, and that each member will have the same voice in all decisions as every other member.

With a small syndicate as with yourself alone there should be that unbreakable rule about understanding everything before any decision becomes final or anything is signed. With five people, it may take five times as long for everybody to be clear on every detail, but it also reduces considerably the chances of something being overlooked—and maybe everything will end up being five times as clear.

How to invest in real estate without buying property: second mortgages and real estate investment trusts

A good deal of the lending by commercial banks and practically all by savings and loan associations is on real estate. It is almost all on first mortgages; second mortgages are handled by companies set up for special lending situations —and quite often by individuals.

Interest on a second mortgage can and usually does go as high as 10%. The reason is supposed to be that the risk is greater: if the borrower defaults on the first mortgage, whoever holds it may sell the property to recover the balance due, but there is no obligation to see that the holder of the second gets anything. This is true, but the law provides the second mortgagee a way to keep this from happening. To use it involves laying out some cash, but this is an excellent investment if the property was worth lending money on in the first place.

Actually, the chief reason for the high rate is that a person borrowing on a second mortgage really needs the money and is resigned to paying a high price for it. It usually isn't for a large sum, so the payments have an easy look to them, and anyway, it's only for five years—or seven at most.

People don't often borrow as little as $1000 on a second mortgage, but it does happen. When they want to do that, they are likely to put an advertisement in one of the business classifications of their local paper. Sometimes a real estate broker will know of someone like that.

With your $1000, you are not going to be able to spend any extra money, so for you there is the very real risk that the borrower may not be able to keep up his payments. To make a judgment on this, you have to know, to begin with, how much he owes on the first mortgage. Then you should learn what his credit rating is if it is available. If he seems to you to be carrying too heavy a load for his income, or if his future looks uncertain, even 10% would make the loan a bad investment.

It is more probable that you would find an opportunity for your $1000 in a discounted second mortgage. "Discounted" means that the holder is willing to transfer the debt for a payment of less than its face value. For example, someone holds a second mortgage for $2000 and is willing to transfer it to you if you will pay $1000. In certain circumstances this could be a very good investment, always assuming that the person owing the money is a good credit risk.

Mortgages are usually "amortized," which means literally to put to death. This is done by monthly payments, which include interest and a sum to reduce the principal. In the beginning the payments include more interest than principal, but as time goes on the interest content goes down and the principal factor goes up. This is somewhat complicated to figure on your scratch pad, but a computer can do it without breathing hard and if such things interest you, a real estate broker will show you an amortization table that will break it down to the penny.

Let's suppose a five-year second mortgage for $2000 is offered to you after it has been in force for two years. If you took it over at that point and held it for the remaining three years of its life, you would get about $1600, which is your $1000 plus $200 each year. This a yield of 20%.

Twenty percent interest is extraordinary; your instinct might tell you to be suspicious. How can such things happen?

Well, it often happens like this. A man is selling a property, and the buyer, after making a down payment and assuming a first mortgage, is still short of the purchase price. The seller is eager to get the deal closed, so he takes a second mortgage for $2000. He doesn't have to put up any money for this—it is simply cash he is not getting on the sale of his house. But he will get monthly payments, which will include interest just as if it were interest on cash he had loaned. If he holds the second mortgage for the full five years, he'll end up with the $2000 he didn't get at the time his house was sold, plus about $670.

But suppose after two years he has to move for some reason. Keeping track of the mortgage would be a nuisance if it had to be done at a distance. If he can transfer the debt for $1000, he has his $2000 plus more than $60—and his only reason for taking the second mortgage at all was to get his house sold. So he discounts it—and you can make some money. Always remembering that it is a good idea to check on the borrower's credit credentials.

In 1960, Congress opened the field of real estate investment to what might be called supersyndicates by passing the Real Estate Investment Trust Act. A real estate investment trust is an unincorporated organization that sells shares to the public and thus can have thousands of people contributing money to be invested in real estate and sharing in the profits. The difference between an REIT and a corporation is chiefly in the fact that a corporation is taxed on its profits before it distributes any to its shareholders, whereas an REIT must distribute 90% of its earnings each year and is not taxed on that money. Shareholders in corporations and REITs have to pay taxes on what they get.

There are four kinds of REITs you can invest in: equity, short-term mortgage, long-term mortgage, and a variety that operates across the board.

An equity REIT goes in primarily for ownership of such

things as shopping centers, large apartment and office buildings, and motels. It will probably put a small part of its assets
into mortgages, but most of its income will be from rentals.
From these, it pays off mortgages and thus increases the
equity that shareholders have in the various properties. If
the value of a property goes up, as it is almost certain to do if
the trust managers know their business, and it is sold, the profits are distributed to the shareholders, and they pay taxes on
them as capital gains—usually long-term.

One of the attractions of an equity REIT is the tax shelter
it can provide through the depreciation allowance. Suppose,
as a shareholder in an equity trust, you are part owner of an
apartment house that cost $1 million. The trust gets $150,000
a year in rentals. Maintenance and property taxes come to
$60,000, and we'll say the annual mortgage payments are
$10,000—$7250 interest and $2750 principal. The income mi-
nus expenses is called cash flow, and it is at least 90% of this
that the trust must distribute to its shareholders. On the apartment house we are talking about, it comes to $72,000.

But 5% of what the apartment house cost is theoretically put
aside each year to build a new one when it is no longer usable;
5% of $1 million is $50,000, and since the law doesn't insist
that this *really* go into a replacement fund, it can be added to
the other tax deductions. By the time all the arithmetic is over,
the shareholders end up having to pay taxes on only thirty-
seven cents out of every dollar they get.

A mortgage REIT specializes in either the long- or short-
term variety, although as a matter of fact most mortgage trusts
have some of both in their portfolios. All REITs borrow to
supplement what they get from their shareholders, and the
way the money structure is set up in this country makes it possible for a well-run trust to borrow from a commercial bank at
the prime rate of interest, which is always the lowest available and is what banks charge their best customers—"best"
being those to whom loans involve the least risk.

Having borrowed the money, our mortgage trust lends it.
Long-term loans are paid off as you amortize a mortgage on
your house—it can take twenty-five to thirty years. The short-

term or interim mortgage has a much higher interest rate—
up to 14% as this is being written—and usually runs for only a
year or eighteen months. Money on this kind of mortgage is
also called a construction and development loan.

C&D loans are made to companies in the business of con-
structing shopping centers, condominiums, apartment houses,
office buildings—or anything else that involves having to pay
out large amounts of money as they go along. The reason for
the high rate of interest is supposed to be the risks in projects
like that. Strikes, unexpected shortage of materials, long spells
of weather when no work can be done can hold a builder back;
theoretically he may not be able to complete the job at all.
This happens very rarely and, when it does, the lender and
the borrower get together and work out something satisfactory to both. It would have to be a pretty foolhardy project
to begin with for the lender to lose money.

Shares in real estate investment trusts can be bought in the
stock market, and they have become very popular in recent
years. Investors have flocked to them because they have provided a yield of from 7% to 10% and because as a group during the past four years they have done better, as far as price
per share is concerned, than the thirty stocks in the Dow Jones
Industrial Average. The trust managers like them because
there is usually a management fee of 1% to 1½% of the total
assets per year, and the assets of trusts range from $10 million
to $400 million.

Prices of REITs fluctuate like the prices of other stocks on
the market, but that shouldn't bother you if you invest in a
trust that is sound. The chief risk is in the number of new
trusts coming on the scene: as of mid-1971 there were 113
operating; by October there were 143, and trusts offering
shares totaling $500 million were in registration with the SEC.
This is a boom, and in all booms there are bound to be fatali-
ties. Some of the newcomers will fail because management
hasn't got the experience or established reputation for ex-
pertise it needs to borrow money at low rates. Some may be
able to borrow the money but won't be able to find places to
lend it all. In that situation, interest has to be paid, and if the

money is just sitting there, the effect is rather as if it were eating itself. This keeps the trust from earning money and, when earnings go down, obviously so do distributions to shareholders. Investors shy away from such a trust, and its shares become worth less and less.

But you can avoid the risky ones. Your first step, if you are interested in this kind of investment, should be to look at the current REIT prices in the Transactions on the New York Stock Exchange or the American Stock Exchange, which are listed in *The Wall Street Journal* and the larger metropolitan dailies. You want to buy as many shares as you can with your $1000, so you should consider as possibilities those quoted at under $20.

Next, compute what the yield on your investment will be. There will be a figure immediately to the right of the company name, which will be the dividend paid most recently. For example, there was a trust selling in November 1971 at $8.50 a share and paying a dividend of $1.00 a year. Divide $1.00 by $8.50 and you have .117—or 11.7% yield, which is very good if everything else is all right.

To find out if it is, you will have to have more information. This will be in a volume of Standard & Poor's Stock Reports, which are in all stockbrokers' offices and in many banks. Your interest is chiefly in how the trust has performed since it was established, and it should be at least five years old for its record to mean anything unless you have a great deal of specialized knowledge about real estate. The trust's record of income and earnings after expenses should be steadily upward. Since it has to pay 90% of its earnings to shareholders, the dividend record will be on a corresponding rise. Its per-share prices should show a history of growth.

REITs operate on a multimillion-dollar scale, and that kind of real estate can be so complicated that only experts can understand the finer points. Recently REITs have been coming on the market sponsored by large banks or insurance companies, which have also always been big lenders on real estate. These are less likely to have the borrowing troubles sometimes besetting the newer, untried trusts: they can borrow at the lowest rates because the officers of the trust management company are also officers of the real estate departments of the sponsoring organization. Thus, the managers of BankAmerica Realty Investors can get just about as much money as they need from the Bank of America—and at the prime rate. This isn't necessarily monopolistic, because a bank or insurance company is just as willing to lend on the same terms to any trust at all provided it can present convincing evidence that it has highly expert management, which many independent trusts are able to do.

All things considered, the investor inexperienced in real estate is probably better off in an REIT that has a powerful bank or insurance company behind it. You don't have to concern yourself with its performance statistics: such a trust is born with a successful record—the sponsor's.

THE STOCK MARKET

*How to think like
a sophisticated investor*

The stock market can offer a number of ways for your $1000 to make money, provided you have a firm grasp on a few fundamental truths. People sometimes get the idea that the market is something it is not, and this error drastically reduces their chances of making money—and opens the way to losing it.

The stock market means all the thousands of stocks that can be bought and sold on the various exchanges and over-the-counter. The New York Stock Exchange is the most influential part of the market place and is what most people have in mind when they say "the market." It is not a living organism with emotions and moods, although you often hear that it is "strong" or "exuberant" or "cautious" or even "depressed." Such adjectives apply not to the market but to what seems to be the prevailing spirit of the people who are buying and selling in it.

You'd think this was too obvious to make a point of, but people often lose sight of it, and when they do they lose money. Whenever there is a general price drop, invariably a lot of stockholders sell because they think something is wrong with the market itself, whereas all that has happened is that a lot of people want to sell at the same time. Usually they are selling for the same reason, and the reason may have nothing to do with the true value of the stocks they are getting rid of. The result is that a lot of good issues are sold and the prices go down, and the traders who can think calmly pick up the bargains.

Everybody knows that the law of the stock market is the law of supply and demand. More buyers than sellers sends prices up; when sellers are dominant, prices go down. The hitch is that the reason for either may not actually be very sound. One autumn day in 1971 an official of a company that was the largest in its industry told a reporter that earnings were going to be down for the current quarter. That would have been enough to drop his company's stock two or three points in any case, but he added that if they were having trouble the rest of the industry must be having a lot worse. On no more evidence than that, stockholders throughout the entire industry started to sell. The industry was tied in with others, so people with those stocks got spooked too. It became a small stampede—and that day the market was "off" substantially.

There are two points of view toward the market: the fundamental and the technical. The fundamentalist concentrates on forming an accurate evaluation of a stock: he buys into a company he is convinced is sound and holds his shares until he sees evidence that dividends will fall off or that the growth limit has been reached. The technician buys or sells according to movements of the market in general, correlated with the price movements of the stocks he is interested in. He knows that the market will move generally up or down over long periods; he knows that in a bull market there can be setbacks lasting as long as a month, and rallies of the same duration in a bear market. Charts are the technician's icons; he chants of tops and bottoms, of supports and breakouts—and there is much to be learned from what he says.

The technical approach has most to offer the trader who

plays the swings in the market. With $1000, you will be able to speculate in part of the market, but you need more than that to be a swinger in common stocks. Where they are concerned, your approach should be primarily fundamental, but you should never lose sight of the technical because even the soundest stocks will move with the tides.

The Rothschilds, who were almost legendary financiers in the eighteenth century, acted on the principle that it was well to buy a property *of known value* (our italics) when others wanted to sell, and to sell when others wanted to buy. This is as wise today as it was two hundred years ago, and even more difficult to live by. There can sometimes be an almost irresistible pull in the opposite direction, particularly for someone new to the market with a relatively small amount of money to put into it. A person in that situation as a rule buys stock when other stocks are going up, keeps it for what he feels is a reasonable profit, then sells. If the price keeps rising, he consoles himself that he wasn't greedy. Often he buys near the top, and soon there are a few days when the price holds steady. It may slip a point or so. Then a lot of shares are sold all over the market—and the point becomes two or three. The investor holds on because he knows a good stock will always come back. If the selling gains momentum, he begins to be uneasy—maybe the stock wasn't as good as he thought. He holds on while prices are sliding to the point where even some of the blue chips are affected. When he has lost eight or nine points, he is sure he made a mistake and sells out to save something from the disaster. It doesn't help when the stock starts back up, as it is almost certain to do if it is really sound.

It can go the other way too. Unless you keep close watch on your stock and the market as a whole, a bull market, when all you hear is that the Dow Jones Industrial Average is going up and up and up, is likely to induce a state of euphoria in which you can overlook the fact that the company you have your money in could be quietly going broke.

As far as what it "does" is concerned, the stock market is the Dow Jones Industrial Average. To say that the market is up or off a certain number of points means that the Dow is up or off. The Average is only one of several indicators, but it is the most convenient because it is computed and published every hour; and it is actually a pretty reliable reflection of general market behavior. However, it is based on 30 New York Stock Exchange stocks, and more than 1700 are listed there, so you must keep in mind that, though a majority move with the Average, there are almost always a couple of hundred that don't—and one of those may be yours.

In order to get into the stock market, you will have to deal with a broker, so it is as important to understand him or her as it is to understand the market.

(A number of brokers are women, but their ratio to men is about 1 to 50. Women take the same examination men do to become registered representatives—the official designation for brokers—and once they have passed, they are compensated by the firms they work for just as men are. However, since men do outnumber women, and since it is a bother to keep saying "he or she" and "him or her," the broker will hereinafter be assumed to be male.)

All brokers are required to know a great deal about the world of finance, but the wisdom they bring to their knowledge varies with the individual just as it does in any other profession. Most brokers have a strong sense of responsibility to their clients. This is practical as well as idealistic: a broker who does the best possible job for his customers is bound to have more customers.

Every buy or sell transaction carries with it a commission to the firm, and the individual broker gets a percentage of it. The commission is based on the amount of money involved, so even with the surcharge on orders of fewer than 1000 shares, what you will buy with your $1000 won't mean more than $35. Brokers being human, the response you get won't be as joyous as it would be if you opened your account with orders totaling $20,000 or $30,000. However, in nearly every office there is at least one young broker fresh from training: brimming with knowledge, bubbling with energy and ambition—and maybe a bit hungry. So unless you already know a broker or have been referred to one, your wisest course is probably to look for one who is just getting started.

Begin your search in a brokerage house you know has a large and experienced research department. Even the most sophisticated people in the market never outgrow their need for reliable information or their appetite for soundly based opinion; where these are available, you can have both at no extra charge. If the firm you decide on has no branch in the town where you live, there is almost certain to be one not more than an hour's drive away. After you open an account, you'll be carrying on practically all your business by telephone anyway.

Call the office first and ask the receptionist if you may speak to one of the younger brokers—if she thinks this is eccentric, she won't say so. Explain to the voice you will hear in a moment that you want to open an account. He'll say to come in and see him, and your next step is to arrange an appointment for a specific time, preferably after market hours. Be sure you do this, even if you live around the corner. If you go into an office cold, you are what the brokers call a "walk-in." It sounds like a butcher's refrigerator—and anyway it's always better to be expected.

One of the rules the brokerage business tries to live by is "Know your customer," so in that first meeting your broker will probably want to chat for a while before you get down to business. We have already stipulated that your $1000 is and will be unattached, but if the broker has been well trained, he will say something about your investment objective—"the investment program that is right for you." Be patient and wait till he has said what he has to say. The point that you must get over to him is that you know exactly what you want to do.* This is important, because unless you are completely sure of yourself, right here is where any plans for your $1000 in the stock market could break down.

Opening a brokerage account involves filling out a form

---

* How you arrive at this knowledge will be the subject of subsequent chapters.

on which you give much the same information about yourself you would give when opening a charge account with a store. At a store, however, your first purchase probably wouldn't be for eight or nine hundred dollars, whereas in the stock market it is quite likely to be. Furthermore, you are not establishing credit with the broker; you are giving data to be used in determining your financial accountability. Your broker will ask if the account is to be margin or cash: you say cash—the legal minimum for a margin account is $2000. You'll be expected to pay at least half the price of what you are going to buy at the time you give the order. The balance will have to be paid within five days.

If you are a married woman, in some states you will have to have your husband's consent to have the account. This is true even if you work and contribute your salary to the family budget. However, if you explain that the money you want to spend in your new account was yours before you were married or became yours afterward as a gift or bequest or by any other method outside the family context, your husband's consent won't be required.

Once you become a customer, you can arrange to have the firm's market letters sent to you—and you should keep up with their special reports. But long before the first meeting with your broker, you will have studied the company whose stock you intend to buy and done a certain amount of supplemental reading in publications like *The Wall Street Journal* or *Barron's* or *Forbes*. You will have seen advisory services advertised and maybe you will have looked at one or two and found them helpful though not to be followed slavishly.

If you have done all that, there is no reason why your broker shouldn't accept you as sophisticated even if you've never actually owned a share of stock before. Sophistication is nothing more complicated than being completely at ease with the world you are operating in.

Chiefly for
the bargain hunter

Even though you don't take your $1000 into the stock market as part of an investment program, you ought to have something definite in mind. There are three options:

1. You can take a course that will bring you better than 5% income and the possibility of capital gain and yet keep the risk almost as low as it would be in a savings account.

2. You can find a stock that is undervalued by the market and will therefore gain more swiftly than others in a rising market and will yield ground more slowly when other prices are falling. If you chart this course carefully, the risk need not be very great.

3. You can use leverage in certain areas that are generally considered entirely speculative. Here it is also possible to reduce the risk.

The third group we will discuss in later chapters. Here we will mention 1 briefly and concentrate on 2.

In the minimum-risk group are preferred stocks and common stocks of companies that are so structured into the economy that it is almost impossible to imagine life without them.

(Technically, bonds are in this class, but they will not be covered here, because with $1000 you would be able to buy only one and it is so difficult to buy just one bond that the small extra yield you would get over a savings account would hardly be worth the trouble. You will hear convertible bonds spoken of sometimes as the ideal investment: a high degree of safety with the possibility of capital gain—but they are of interest only to investors with larger sums of money.)

The preferred stocks of solidly established companies often have yields well above the savings account level. In late 1971 you could have bought the preferreds of Dupont and General Motors at prices that represented yields of 6.5% each, one of AT&T at 6.5%, and two of Consolidated Edison at 7.2% and 7.5%. And there were many others like them.

Such preferred stocks are usually at a price where you couldn't own more than 20 shares with your $1000 and more probably only 10 or 15. Since their prices don't fluctuate much, you wouldn't expect a rise of more than five points or so. Ordinarily, people who buy preferreds plan to hold them for the sake of the income for a number of years.

You have a better chance of price appreciation with the common stocks of such companies, and they are pretty safe too. In 1971 you could have bought 20 shares of AT&T for $1000, and the dividend would have given you a 6.3% yield. Or you could have had 40 shares of Con Edison with a yield of 7.2%. You can find others in this range by combing the daily exchange transactions in the newspapers.

Of course, dividends on common stock are not guaranteed as they are on preferreds; but on the positive side is the fact that the directors of a well-known company hate to lower a dividend or pass one altogether. Furthermore, common stocks with good dividends are likely to go up in price. It even happens sometimes that, when the price goes so high that people who own shares of it and want to sell have a hard time finding buyers, the company will split the stock. If you own 40 shares and there is a two-for-one split, you suddenly own 80 shares and you haven't had to spend any more money. The price always goes down after a split, but with a good company it starts climbing again. Of course you can't count on a stock being split, but if it is paying good dividends right along, holding it is worth while because it can give you a good return on your money with very little risk. You should always keep your eye on it and on the market but, with a company like AT&T or General Motors, a drop of a few points in price shouldn't alarm you.

A bargain, in the stock market or anywhere else, is something worth more than you pay for it. This is another one of those statements so obvious that you don't bother thinking about it, but you should. The key word is "worth." A low-priced stock isn't necessarily a bargain: it might really be undervalued or it just might not be much good. It's up to you to find out which it is.

There are real bargains at almost all prices, but the lower the price the more room there is to move up. This suits your $1000, because when you buy a stock selling under $20 a share you'll be able to buy from 50 to 100 shares, so that every time the price goes up one point your profit will be from $50 to $100.

Your broker will probably tell you, if you show an inclination toward a stock in this range, that it is speculative and that he feels it his duty to warn you against it. This doesn't necessarily mean he thinks the stock is no good; it is simply that he knows it is not the most conservative investment and doesn't want to be suspected of having tried to sell you on it.

There are several tests of a genuine bargain. The first one you can make from the figures in the New York Stock Exchange, the American Exchange, and the Over-the-Counter transactions in *The Wall Street Journal* or a large metropolitan daily. Local papers don't usually give the prices of more than a few over-the-counter stocks, and sometimes they include companies whose only claim to inclusion is that they are local too.

To the right of the company's name will be a figure showing

the last dividend paid. Divide this by the price you would have to pay for the stock and you will have the yield. Over-the-counter stocks are quoted "bid and asked." The bid price is approximately what you get when you sell; asked is about what you pay to buy. As you might expect, asked is always higher—and it is what you use to find the yield. This is your first clue to an undervalued stock.

"Undervalued" means that for some reason traders and investors have failed to see the real present worth and future potential of the stock and haven't created a demand for it that would send its price up. One thing people in the market look for is an attractive dividend yield. This doesn't in itself necessarily mean a good stock, but it is a logical point to start investigating from. An hour's browsing through the price lists will show you several dozen with yields better than 5%.

On the whole, you will probably do better with a company making a product you know something about or offering a service you are familiar with. If you can't deduce from the company's name what it does, you will find the information in its Standard & Poor's Stock Report. This is where you will look for your next clues.

You will find these Stock Reports in any brokerage office, many banks, and some public libraries. You'll have to ask to be directed to them, but most places will let you take all the time you need to study them.

A Stock Report covers both sides of a 9 x 6¼-inch page and is easy to understand. You will find the dividends the company has paid during the past ten years. They should show a steady upward trend. There should be at least five raises in that time, and if dividends have stayed the same for more than two years, this should be at the top and during the most recent years.

Another column will show the company's earnings. These should also show a steady increase.

Usually the Report includes the price/earnings ratio for the past ten years, but if you can't find it, there will be data you can compute it from. The present price of the stock divided by the most recently reported earnings per share will give you the ratio. This is what a broker refers to when he says, "So-and-so is selling at 20 times earnings" or "So-and-so is at a 15 multiple." There is some difference of opinion among the experts about how far you can stretch the significance of the p/e, but there is no doubt that Wall Street regards earnings as the life-blood of a company. This being so, the price/earnings ratio is its blood pressure. An undervalued stock will have a low p/e—probably under 15.

Somewhere in the Report there will be figures headed "Balance Sheet," and among them you will find *net working capital*. This refers to the current assets of the company (as opposed to fixed assets—buildings, equipment, and so on) minus the current liabilities—money coming in minus what has to be paid out right away, or pretty soon. Clearly, if all the money coming in had to be paid out immediately, the company would be in trouble because there would be nothing left over for day-to-day expenses. The difference between these two figures is called *net working capital*.

Now when you buy stock in a company you are literally buying a share in the ownership of everything it has—buildings, machinery, land, as well as the cash it has in the bank and whatever is going to be turned into cash. You even own part of the company's debts, because the interest on bonds and the dividends on preferred stock have to be paid before you can share in the profits.

So when you have the figure for the *net working capital*, look in the bottom right-hand corner of the second side of the Report and under the heading "Capitalization" you will find the number of shares of common stock outstanding. Divide this into the working capital and if the result is equal to or more than the price the stock is selling for, the stock is likely to be a bargain. The stockholders are getting ownership of all the assets of the company but are actually paying only for the working capital. This doesn't often happen, but when it does, it is like getting possession of a house by paying only the current living expenses of the family occupying it.

In summary, the five principal clues to an undervalued stock are:

1. a dividend that represents a yield of 5% or more, based on the price you will have to pay;

2. a general increase in dividends over the past ten years, with at least five definite increases;

3. the same pattern in earnings;

4. a price/earnings ratio of 15 or under;

5. a net working capital-per share figure that is equal to or more than the price of the stock at the time you are thinking about buying it.

To see how this works out in practice, let's look at the stock of a real company. Since the purpose here is not advertising, we'll disguise it as the Wehaul Transportation Company.

In 1970 the stock was selling at one time for $13. The dividend was $1.00. This was a yield of slightly better than 7.6%. Affirmative on Point 1.

From 1962 to 1967 the dividends climbed steadily from 51¢ a share to $1.00. From 1967 to 1970 the figure held at $1.00 and indications were that it would be the same for 1971. Affirmative on Point 2.

Earnings rose from 95¢ a share in 1962 to $1.44 in 1967. In 1968 they dropped to $1.34, but the next year they started up again without interruption until 1970. Figures for 1971 were not available as this is written. A qualified affirmative on Point 3.

The price/earnings ratio was 9 when the price was at 13. Highly affirmative on Point 4.

The *net working capital* divided by the number of common stock shares gave the quotient 5. And the price of the stock was 13. Negative on Point 5.

If you had bought Wehaul at the 1970 low, your $1000 would have paid for 75 shares, including commissions. The 1971 high, before the slide that began in early September, was 25½. If you had sold at that point you would have had a profit of about $875, plus the 7.6% income on your money while you were holding the stock. When the market started downhill in September, Wehaul went with it, but you might well have held on, because what you read in the Stock Report would have convinced you that the company had a fairly bright future—and it was still paying the same dividend. By mid-December, when the market was having a rally, Wehaul had started back up.

The five points together represent an ideal. A stock may be negative on one or more of them and still be a bargain, although there could be enough things you can't be certain about for it to be called speculative.

Take dividends, for instance. When a company is new in its field, it may need all the money it can get to generate momentum, so it retains earnings and, as the saying is on Wall Street, plows them back into operations: production, research, or sales. Sometimes a company in this situation will pay a very small dividend as a sort of signal that it is on its way to doing better, but even when there is no dividend at all, if it is attractively priced, it may be worth your while to apply other tests.

You may already be familiar with what the company does. If you're not, the Stock Report will tell you and even add details about how well it has been doing it and what its prospects are in general. You will have to make your own decision about whether it will continue to do it well enough to send the price of the stock up.

How can you come to a conclusion about that? It isn't easy. Looking back, you might feel now that some years ago you would have foreseen the importance of air conditioning or computers in our lives and would have put money into companies involved in them at a time when their stocks would have been bargains. But would you have forecast the recent popularity of mobile homes or pollution control? Even if you had guessed right about the industries, not all the individual companies in them succeeded. One reason a company just starting out must be regarded as speculative is that, even if there is a demand for the product or service it sells, it is difficult to know whether the demand will hold up and even harder to be sure the individual company is going to be able to meet it.

If a company is fairly new, it won't have enough of a record to base a reliable opinion on, so you will have to find out something about its management. For all the talk about figures, companies are people. Who are the people running this company? Not only the directors, but the officers in charge of production, sales, research, advertising. What is their background? Why did they join this company and what is their experience? What do they say their plans are and do they have the right motivation to carry them out?

The company's annual report will give you some information on these points. You will have to write to the public relations officer and ask for it, and you will not be surprised that it says nice things about management. The essential facts, however, will be there, and often you will be able to get a more objective opinion from a specialist in your broker's research department. If you are satisfied that management is smart and aggressive, and if the company's product or service seems to meet more than adequately a demand that looks as if it would continue, the stock is probably a bargain. This can be true even if dividends are negligible or non-existent when you buy it.

A sag in earnings is not in itself a reason to reject a stock—at least until you know the reason. Of course, if the company lost money by not keeping up its quality standard or by failing to meet competition in its market, there is nobody to blame but management. Often you find that after a period of lower earnings there is a transfusion of new blood, and while everybody hopes that will have a good effect, you can't be sure for some time. You may feel sure from what you learn that the new people will do well and that the stock may be worth buying, but if you buy it in these circumstances, you will be speculating.

You realize how important it is to have reliable information when you understand that even with the best management earnings can have a setback. A strike can do it. A sudden shift in public taste can result in some discouraging figures. *The Wall Street Journal* had a story one day in 1971 about companies that had stocked up on striped bell-bottoms because that was what all the kids were wearing. Then, for no reason anybody could see, the younger generation started demanding solid colors—and stripes were out. This was tough on earnings for a time and the very best management might not have gone so heavy on stripes, but you can't put too much blame on the ones who did.

The price/earnings ratio of a low-priced stock is not likely to be high, but if it is above 25 you should be skeptical, especially if the record shows a fairly rapid rise to that point. Price/earnings has nothing at all to do with what a stock is actually worth; it tells only what people in the market feel about it—feel, you will note, not think. It sometimes happens that a stock generates such market enthusiasm that it is subjected to almost no thought at all. People buy and buy with great exuberance, and the price keeps going up. Then one day the multiple, as Wall Street calls it, gets up around 40 or 50, and somebody suddenly realizes that the balance sheet nowhere near justifies the price. He sells and, as soon as somebody else sees why, there is more selling, and the price drops— usually a lot faster than it rose.

The figures in a company's balance sheet—as shown in the Standard & Poor's Stock Report—are worth a close look. A stock can be a bargain even if it isn't affirmative on Point 5: a *net working capital*-per share figure that is equal to or more than the current price of the stock. Conversely, even if this is affirmative, there may be factors that would tell you to be cautious.

The details are in the components of what is called the company's *current ratio*. This is the ratio between its *total current assets* and its *total current liabilities*. Most analysts agree that a healthy current ratio is 2 to 1. This means that during the coming year the company will have twice as much money coming in as it is going to have to pay out on obligations it has already contracted for. The surplus is the *net working capital* referred to in Point 5—the money a company has available for day-to-day operations and, incidentally, to grow on.

The components of current liabilities don't make much difference. They represent money management knows has to be paid out no matter what. But the items on the balance sheet that make up current assets can tell you things you might overlook if you just read the total. These items are *cash, market-able securities, accounts receivable,* and *inventories.*

Cash is obvious—money at present in the bank.

Theoretically, marketable securities can be turned into cash within five days. Presumably, management has invested in sound securities, but even bonds go down in price, and in a long market slump the company would lose money on this item if it had to convert into cash.

Accounts receivable are monies that are owing to the company. You hope it isn't carrying a lot of deadheads on the books, and the assumption is that receivables will become cash eventually, but they can't be spent right now. Also, accounts receivable have to be judged in the light of what the company does. A loan company wouldn't have anything but; at the other extreme, utilities have none that last very long—if you don't pay your bills, service is shut off. To a company that is a supplier to other companies, accounts receivable would be very important indeed. The balance sheet figures in a Stock Report are always for two years, and you should look on any increase in receivables from one year to the next as a signal to proceed with caution.

The same is true of inventories. Utilities and transportation companies don't have them, but to companies that make things to sell or whose business is selling, they can mean a great deal.

Inventories are product not yet sold, but the term also includes raw material not yet turned into product and material in the process of being manufactured. The figures in the balance sheet next to *net sales* should obviously be larger than the one next to inventories—how much larger depends on what the nature of the business is. There is no rule of thumb as to what this ratio should be, but one thing is for sure: it is a bad sign if it is lower this year than it was last.

Money in inventories, accounts receivable, and securities represent money tied up—not seriously perhaps, but still not liquid. The report on the New England Pump Company (another fictitious name for a real company) shows a current ratio of 2.5 to 1, which is excellent. But it also notes that inventories accounted for 49% of current assets and receivables for 45%, while cash was only 3.7%. This is a picture of a company that could be in a bit of a bind if there were a sudden demand for cash.

There are other signs in the two-year balance sheet figures. Have net sales fallen? What about operating costs? Lower net sales and higher operating costs can be a serious squeeze on profits.

Finally, all these figures should be compared with those of other companies in the same industry. They are your company's competition, and your company has to stack up well against them or the stock isn't a bargain at any price.

We have been assuming that your bargains have been priced low enough for you to buy 50 or 100 shares. Any transaction under 100 shares is an odd lot and an odd lot costs more to buy or sell than a round lot, or 100 shares. A charge called the *odd lot differential* is added to the regular commission—12½¢ per share on stocks selling under 55 and 25¢ a share on stocks over that. (It's over and under 40 on the American Exchange.) Sometimes there are bargains in relatively higher-priced stocks that more than make up for the differential.

On November 2, 1971, for example, a stock in the communications industry was mentioned in *The Wall Street Journal* in a way that sounded as if it might be a bargain. It was selling at 73 and you could have bought 10 shares. You wouldn't have had that round-lot exhilaration of knowing you've made $100 every time the stock goes up a point, but by the first week of January '72 this stock was at 125 and you would have had a profit of $520 before commissions.

Or you could buy two odd lots of the low-priced issues. It is just as well not to own more than two even if you have plenty of money to spend. You should never invest in anything you can't keep your eye on, and two is about the limit you can deal with adequately unless you've had a lot of experience.

Whether you are dealing in odd lots or round lots, when you buy and when you sell are important. The best time to buy is when the stock is at the absolute bottom, and the best time to sell is at the very top—and nobody in the world can tell when either will be or recognize it when it happens. However, there are favorable low points and high points that are possible to see.

There are two clues to a good buying time: one in the market as a whole and one in the price range of the stock you are considering. If it is a low-priced stock and you have concluded that it is an authentic bargain, the range isn't important: the price is low because it *is* undervalued. In the case of a higher-priced stock, look at the Stock Report. Somewhere you will find the price ranges for previous years. They won't all be the same, but you may find that they follow a pattern, with the highs and lows at the same general level. If it is a stock that moves only five or six points a year, you won't get much action for the part of your $1000 you put into it. If you find a strong issue with a wider range, buy near the low for the current year if you can—or, if the year is still young, the low for the previous year.

But this can only be a guide. In a declining market, even a good stock can fall beyond its low for this year or last. Since there is no sense in buying a stock when the price is going down, how can you tell when it reaches bottom?

You can't. You can't recognize the bottom until *after* it has been reached, and you know that has happened only when the price starts moving up.

Here again use caution—and watch the market in general. There are times when it seems wishy-washy: it doesn't move strongly either up or down. This usually happens after a fairly long decline; there is a rally, the averages will go up a few points, then sag again. Your stock may go up a point or so, then stop, and maybe slip back. When the market begins to show strength, watch the price of your stock in relation to how many shares are sold. If it closes on its high for the day and the volume is up from the day before, and if this happens a couple of days in succession, it is likely to be a safe time to buy.

The same relationship can help at the selling end. If your stock sags and closes at its low for the day and the volume of sales is up from the previous day, it is a warning sign. This isn't likely to happen with a good stock until after it has been on a rise for some time, but if and when there are two or three days like that, you should think about selling.

You should keep track of your company's earnings all the time you own the stock, but remember that the figures alone don't tell the whole story. Earnings can increase when a company keeps ahead of its competition with new and improved products supported by smart, aggressive merchandising and sales practices—or they can be made to *seem* to increase according to what accounting methods the company uses. Earnings are so important that companies are sometimes tempted to use accounting methods that present a more favorable earnings picture than the facts justify.

If the figures show your company's earnings going up, be sure to read its annual reports for a couple of years back—if there are realistic reasons for the rise in earnings, you can be sure they'll be there. If you can't find the facts, just the figures in the balance sheet, it would be a good idea to investigate further. When figures are without solid foundation, sooner or later the market uncovers the fact, and the selling starts.

The secret of profits in the stock market is to cut your losses and let your profits run. Until you get used to it, anything you do in the market will require courage. No matter how uninhibited your $1000 may be, it is still important money, and you don't commit it lightly to anything. One thing you need to be certain you're honest with yourself about—that you are not buying or selling because someone else tells you to or because a lot of other people are doing the same thing. If your decision is based on the best information you can get and if you are satisfied that it is adequate, go ahead whether everybody else agrees with you or not. You can accept it as an axiom that you can't make money in the stock market by following the crowd.

6

Options:
chiefly for
the speculator

In the stock market, options are supposed to be for the professional speculator only: *warrants* and *puts* and *calls* are mysteries the uninitiated rarely think of asking to have solved. Even *rights* are so little talked about that hundreds of investors get them and could make money on them with no risk at all—and don't, simply because nobody has ever told them how they could. All this is too bad and not really necessary.

With your $1000 you would be unlikely (and unwise) to buy rights, although you could. They come into existence when a company is about to offer a new stock issue to the public: the company gives current stockholders rights to buy the new shares at a price below the present price of the stock already on the market. Stockholders who don't want to use the rights to buy shares may sell them. Often stockholders don't understand that this is possible; sometimes those who do procrastinate or don't read the terms of the rights—and suddenly it is too late, because the lives of rights are short: never longer than a month and often not that long.

You can buy rights just as you do stocks, but they rise in value only when the stock already on the market does, and if the stock goes down, so do the rights—instantly. Because of the short life of rights, to make money, you would have to buy them, have the stock go up, and sell them—all before the expiration date. The risk is too great to make buying them worth while.

Warrants are another matter. A warrant gives the holder the right to buy a stipulated amount of the company's stock at a fixed price until a specified date, which is always at least several years away. Some warrants are forever. They are traded on the various exchanges and over-the-counter, but their resemblance to ordinary securities ends there. Warrants give you no claim on the company the way bonds and preferred stocks do; and no interest or dividend is ever paid on them no matter how much money the company makes. They are simply the right to buy stock.

Your broker isn't likely to tell you so, but with your $1000 you can sometimes make more money in stock warrants than you can in the stocks themselves. For example, if you had bought AT&T warrants at their 1970 low and had sold them at their 1971 high, you would have made $500. The same pattern with AT&T common stock would have earned only $270. This is because with $1000 you could have bought 100 warrants but only 20 shares of stock—and because the warrants went up 71% while the stock was advancing 33%. The reason your broker wouldn't have considered this kind of thing suitable for you is that warrants are considered highly speculative, and his feeling would probably be that if you have limited funds to put into the market you shouldn't speculate.

As we have pointed out, there is no need for you to say that you are limited to $1000, and anyway a warrant takes on some of the investment characteristics of the stock it is tied to. Nobody would call AT&T common stock speculative, and while you can't exactly put AT&T warrants in the widows and orphans category, they certainly shouldn't be called as speculative as warrants tied to volatile stocks.

Let's say that one day in 1972 Bright Horizon, Inc., issues

warrants, each giving the holder the right to buy one share of its common stock for $30 until 1983, and let's say at the time the warrants are issued the stock is selling on the market at 20. Nobody is going to pay $30 for a share of stock that can be bought for $20, but if Bright Horizon is a good company it's worth while holding onto the warrants. In eleven years the stock could easily go well beyond 30—it might go to 50 or 60 or even to 100.

Lots of people don't want to wait that long and the warrants haven't cost them anything, so they offer them for sale to realize a little unexpected profit. If Bright Horizon hasn't had a particularly impressive record of growth so far, the bids won't be very high. With your $1000, you might be able to get them for $2.50 apiece. You could buy 300 and have some cash left over.

Now suppose Bright Horizon moves up. There is good news about the company, and the traders begin to see possibilities. They bid the price up to $3.00 a warrant, then $3.50. If the stock keeps going up, so will the warrants. One day they are selling for $4.50. What do you do? You can hold on for a bigger rise—or you can realize a profit of $600 before commissions right now.

A lot of people will opt for the profit, but a lot will hold on. This is how a market in warrants grows. The significant point is that nobody who buys the warrants expects to exercise them *at that time.* The exercise price plus the premium (what you have to pay to buy the warrants) is always more than the current price of the stock.

If the price of Bright Horizon stock keeps going up, the price of the warrants almost certainly will too. Let's say the stock hits 50. At that point, the warrants will be selling for at least 20: the difference between the exercise price and the price of the stock. This isn't by divine law; it is simply that the true value of the warrant is now $20, and it isn't likely that anybody who owns one would sell it for less. Actually, the price of the warrants would probably be higher.

How long can this kind of thing go on? Only as long as traders think the price of the stock will go higher than the exercise price plus what they have to pay for the warrants. At any moment, for any of dozens of reasons, some of them may decide Bright Horizon won't go that high. They sell warrants, and the price goes down. It is well to keep in mind that, though a warrant gains in price at a greater percentage rate than its stock, the same relationship holds true on the way down.

This difference in pace is leverage, and there is no dependable way to tell before you buy it how much leverage there is in a warrant. You will hear stories that will cause acquisitive prickling at the back of your neck—like if you had put $1000 into Tri-Continental warrants in 1942, you could have sold out in 1969 for well over $2 million. In one four-year stretch, your $1000 would have become $200,000 in RKO warrants; there were two years in which Hoffman Radio warrants would have netted you a half million. There is no record that anybody actually cashed in on those gains—just that they were there to be made. More sobering are the stories of the warrants that went down and became worth nothing at all.

Clearly, the leverage in a warrant tied to a volatile stock is going to pack more excitement than something stodgy, and there isn't much point in buying warrants tied to a stock that hardly moves at all, but there is an area in between where there are well-managed companies competitive in their industries. Stock in any of these is almost sure to move up and if such a one issues warrants and you can buy and sell them at the right time your chances of making money are quite good. The principles of timing in warrants are about the same as they are for stocks.

If you consider warrants, your first job is to find one that looks promising. This isn't as easy as the first step in choosing an undervalued stock, because there is no newspaper that publishes the prices of all warrants being traded. Of the approximately 300 in existence, only about 100 are easily accessible every day, most of them in the American Stock Exchange Transactions. There will be a dozen or so in the New York Stock Exchange lists and a scattered few in the Over-the-Counter. You will recognize the warrant quotation by the lower-case "wt" after the company's name. The warrants are not always listed with the company stock; many on the American Exchange are with companies listed on the NYSE.

(There are signs of change. Trading in warrants is on the increase, and the NYSE says it will report more about them in its statistical reports. If the American follows, it may be that most warrants, instead of the present few, will be quoted.)

What you will find in the present lists is only that there *are* warrants and what they are selling for. To get further necessary information, you have to go back to the Stock Reports. As a matter of fact, if you don't find a warrant in the newspaper that interests you, you can find just about all there are in the volumes of the Standard & Poor's Stock Reports. On the second side of every Report, in the lower right-hand corner, there will be the heading "Capitalization." You can flip the pages quickly, keeping your eye on that spot, until you see in capital letters WARRANTS.

Here you will find the most important things you need to know: the general terms of the warrants. These will be the exercise price, the number of shares available to be bought with the warrants, and the expiration date. It will look something like this: "To buy 761,660 shares at $46.50 a share until October 1, 1977."

The number of shares is the number the company has set aside to meet all the warrants issued if they should be exercised, and it does have some bearing on the price. If the speculators decide they want the warrants, the price is likely to go up faster with a small number than with a large one—supply and demand again.

The number of warrants is particularly important to warrant holders if it is ever increased by a stock split or a stock dividend. When that happens, there should be an adjustment in the exercise terms of the warrant to compensate for it. If there are 1 million shares available for the warrants and the stock is split two for one, there are suddenly 2 million, and with the larger supply people aren't going to have to pay so much for them. The price will go down. This is why you will sometimes see exercise terms like "To buy 1.378 shares for

$25 . . ." Originally, it was 1 share for $25, but the number of shares was increased to avoid dilution.

Often in the Stock Report there will be a note: "Terms and trading basis should be checked in detail," but even if there isn't such a note, you should check. You do this in a *Moody* or *Standard & Poor's Manual*. In the pages devoted to the company you are interested in, there will be a "Capitalization" heading like the one in the Stock Report, and that is where you will find the data on warrants. If the warrants are protected against dilution, the fact will probably be mentioned there, but sometimes there are lags in printing, so you ought to check on the point with your broker before ordering. Very rarely, there will be a warrant that is *callable*, which means that the company has the right to call in any warrants outstanding by paying the holders a specified sum. Unless the call price will give you a profit above what you would have to pay for the warrant, plus commission, there's no point in buying it.

The expiration date is important. As a general rule, it is wise never to hold a warrant that has two years or less to run. In the last two years of a warrant's life, something can easily happen to drive the price of the stock down, even if it is a good stock. The price of the warrant will go down with it—and there may not be time for it to come back up to a profitable level.

To summarize:

Warrants are speculative, but they are not speculative *only* because they are warrants. Any warrant is completely and for all its life inseparable from the stock it is certified to buy. Its speculative elements will be in proportion to those of the stock.

Leverage is inherent in warrants, but there is no realistic way to determine how much. Terms like "leverage ratio" can't be taken as laws or even rules of thumb.

Check all the terms of a warrant before you buy it. And stay away from any warrant that has only two years or less to its expiration date. This should be an unbreakable rule.

About timing—the same guides apply for warrants as for stocks, but keep in mind that warrants respond to general movements of the market to a greater percentage extent than their stocks do—on the way down as well as on the way up. Don't wait too long when there are signals to sell.

Puts and *calls* are options to sell or buy stocks, and they come into existence when people want to buy them and other people are willing, as the technical term is, to *write* them. A call gives you the right, for a sum that varies according to the price of the stock at the time, to buy 100 shares (puts and calls are never for odd lots) at any time within the next thirty, sixty, or ninety days, or six months, at a specified price called the *striking price*. A put is the right to sell in the same way. Calls and puts have a leverage element that makes it possible for you to buy 100 shares by putting up only 20% of the purchase price—which you'd never be able to do with an ordinary margin account. You would also be able to sell short without having to borrow the shares you have to deliver and waiting until the price goes up a fraction of a point, as the SEC insists you must.

Until recently, Wall Street thought nobody should do anything with puts and calls without extensive capital and lots of experience, but the past two years have seen a growing willingness to educate the small investor in these mysteries. As we will show later, there is one way you can make small profits on puts with not a great deal of risk and on calls with practically none. But first the more speculative way.

Let's say you hear that Progress, Inc., is one of four or five companies bidding on a fat government contract. You look into Progress and find that it is a well-managed outfit: you like its balance sheet and the dividends and earnings show a history of healthy growth. But it is selling at 30, and your $1000 will buy only 30 shares.

A call will give you the right to buy 100 shares at 30, and a six-month call would cost you about $600. You buy it—and Progress gets the contract. Six months later the stock has doubled and is now worth 60. With the call in your hand, you'd have no trouble borrowing the cash to pay the $3000 the call lets you pay for the stock. You sell it immediately and out of the $6000 pay back the loan. Your profit is $2400 before commissions and you have used only $600 of *your* money.

This happy ending depends on Progress getting the contract. But maybe it won't. Sound as the company is, the stock probably won't double in six months in ordinary circumstances, and it would have to go at least to 38 for you to break even. It might do that in six months, but suppose it didn't?

Then you don't exercise your call, and you lose your $600.

In buying a call on any stock, your chief problem is finding someone willing to sell you the 100 shares if you exercise the option. The striking price is usually the market price at the time the call is arranged, so the most likely prospect is someone who has been holding the stock for a while and has made a paper profit at the present price. Or somebody who simply has the stock and wants to gamble, paper profit or not.

Your broker will undertake to find such a person for you. His firm may delegate the job to a dealer in puts and calls who either has the stock in his own inventory or knows where he can get it. You must pay cash for the option when it is arranged and of course, if you exercise it, you pay your broker a commission for buying the stock.

When you buy a put, you are paying for the right to sell 100 shares of stock at some time in the future at what the price is at the moment. You wouldn't do this unless you expected the price to go down so you can buy the stock you are going to sell for less than you are going to sell it for. This is selling short without meeting the requirements for a short sale (which you couldn't do anyway with only $1000) and without risking any more than the premium, which is the trade name for what the option costs you.

The price of a call or put can sometimes be negotiated, but as a rule the thirty-day options sell for 10% of the striking price and the six-month options for 20%. The others are around 15%. You can buy a call or put on any security that is traded—even warrants. All that is necessary is to find someone willing to write it.

There is no point in buying it unless you have good reason to believe the stock will move far enough so that your profit will more than cover the premium plus broker's commission. And of course you can't be certain about that. In fact, if you buy a put or a call, you should know that in an estimated 85% of the cases it doesn't happen. That many options are never exercised. For the other 15%, there is that quick leverage into sizable profits.

But what about the 85% that is just sacrificed? Well, maybe "sacrificed" is the wrong word. The money doesn't simply disappear—money never does. It always goes somewhere—in this case into somebody else's pocket, the pocket of the writer of the options.

So how about writing (selling) puts and calls? That's where most of the profit is. With your $1000, you can write a put or a call—maybe several over a period of time—and some of that 85% will come to you.

Let's say you would like to sell a put on Progress, Inc. This means you are willing to give someone else (whom you may never see) the right to sell to *you* 100 shares of Progress at a specified price. Clearly, you will have to have the money to pay for the stock if and when this other person "puts" it to you, so the striking price will have to be $9.00 or less in order to fit into your $1000.

Actually, this is a way to make money buying stock you would like to have anyway—and you shouldn't write a put unless you are satisfied that the stock is good and you would like to have it.

We are assuming you have written a six-month put, so you get about $140 net. If the buyer exercises, you also get 100 shares of a stock you like; if he doesn't, you have the $140 anyway and can write another put.

An even more comfortable transaction would be to sell a call some time after you had bought 100 shares of stock and have seen it go up four or five points. Say you had bought Progress at 9 and now it is at 14, and you write a call with that as the striking price. If the call is for six months, the premium (which you get) will be about $250 after fees—maybe a bit more. But the stock won't be "called" from you unless it goes at least to 17. If it is called, you will have made your profit out of the rise from 9 to 14, plus the $250 for writing the call. And now you have cash to buy more stock. There has been no risk of losing—only the possibility of not making as much as you might have if you had held onto the stock and it had gone up.

Of course, if the price doesn't go to 17, the buyer of the call doesn't exercise it, and you keep the $250 and you still have the stock.

Dealers in puts and calls publish booklets giving what they say are "all" the facts about these options. Since the dealers are in business to make money, they manage to imply that buying or selling puts and calls is only for the wealthy. A booklet will tell you, for example, that to sell a call you should have a portfolio of at least $25,000. They make it sound like a requirement, but it isn't. With a portfolio that size you are likely to get into the habit of writing calls, which is fine for the dealers, but you can sell just one call provided you have the stock to deliver if it is called from you—and you can write just one put if you have the money to buy the stock if the put is exercised.

Time was when a broker would probably have refused to arrange either end of a put or call for an inexperienced investor, especially one without large amounts of money to finance such a project. But change is in the air. When an option is exercised, there are commissions—always two and often three, sometimes four. Consider A, who buys a call—and B, who sells it. If the call is exercised, A buys the stock. One commission for a broker. B has to sell it. One commission for a broker. A may sell right after buying, to realize a profit. One commission for a broker. B (who wouldn't have been you) may have written the call without having the stock to deliver: foolish B now has to buy it in order to sell it. One commission for a broker. Imagine the happiness generated by these commissions if A and B were customers of the same broker.

Brokers are imagining it and that is why, as this is being written, option departments are being rapidly enlarged throughout the brokerage business. As always, the brokers will prefer the large operators to the small. They may tell you you shouldn't speculate in options; they may stress the complications of puts and calls—and their curious combinations with the esoteric names: straddles, spreads, strips, and straps. Unless you take up options as a major occupation, you don't even have to know what they are. The indications are that the near future will provide plenty of scope for action with the simple forms.

Commodities: for speculators only

Commodity trading has been compared with betting on horse races and there are certain similarities, but the analogy fails on one fundamental point. If you make a career of the horses, you will inevitably end up in the red, whereas in commodities it's possible to get into a high tax bracket. The essential difference is in two vital areas: profit and loss. If your money is on a horse that fades in the stretch, you lose it all; if you own a contract of soybeans, for example, and things take a bad turn, you can limit your losses. In fact, if you know what to do, you can lose more than half the time and still make substantial profits; and as for the old saying that you can't go broke taking a profit, there are records of commodity traders taking profits on 90% of their trades and still ending up with staggering losses. In the commodity market, "Cut your losses and let your profits run" is the rule for survival.

With $1000, if you are new to the market, you will be limited in what you can do—which is a good thing, because it simplifies matters. You will be able to buy contracts in job lots

(1000 bushels) of five grains: barley, oats, rye, flax, and rape-seed, and you will have to do it on the Winnipeg Grain Exchange in Canada. The costs of trading on the exchanges in the United States are beyond the scope of your $1000. Later, we will go into the mechanics of trading in Canada if you don't live there.

Commodity exchanges are simply market places in a world grown too big for farmers to carry their harvested crops to town, where they can meet buyers and haggle over prices. A soybean grower in Illinois, for example, doesn't expect to sell his grain directly to a processor. He takes it to his local grain elevator and sells it to the operator, who stores it until *he* can sell it to a processor. If there were no exchanges, every elevator operator would have to negotiate price with every grower, and growers would be put into the position of having to shop around for a fair price. The exchanges record prices and, though these change, everybody knows what the changes are as soon as they happen so that on any given day everybody gets the same.

If the elevator man can sell his grain immediately at a profit, he has no problem. But he can't always find a buyer who wants to use the beans right away, so he contracts with a man who is willing to buy now for future delivery on the chance that before the delivery date the price will go up and he will be able to sell the contract at a profit. This man is a speculator. He doesn't expect to take delivery on the grain: he buys the contract only to sell it. And the elevator man can be sure now that if the price of soybeans goes down he won't lose money.

The speculators perform the same function for processors. A processor wants to figure his costs on future business, and it will help to know the exact price he will have to pay for soybeans when he needs them. A speculator will contract to sell him beans for future delivery at a specified price; he does this because he believes the price will go down on the open market. He doesn't have the beans he sells, but he doesn't have to have them, because the delivery date is well in the future and before then he will buy his contract back—he hopes for less money, and so make a profit.

The speculator in each case takes the risk: the elevator operator and the processor have *hedged* against loss from changes in price. Today there are thousands of speculators. There are uncountable conditions that can effect supply and daily shifts in world situation that can affect demand. They all change the opinions of speculators about what the price of a given commodity will be by certain specified delivery dates, and the speculators buy and sell from and to one another accordingly. With fifty or more commodities on the market, and with the thousands of speculators trying to outguess one another about the future price of each, there is a great deal of action on the commodity exchanges.

There are a number of these. In the United States, the best known is the Chicago Board of Trade, which was made famous by Frank Norris's novel *The Pit*, about trading in wheat futures. There is a pit for each commodity: it is a hexagonal arrangement of steps leading down to a small clear space in the center. Brokers stand there and on the various steps so each one can see all the others, and they signal bids and acceptances for their speculator clients by a complicated set of hand signs and yells so that the trading floor on a busy day is rather like a series of mob scenes all going on at once. But it isn't chaos; the apparent confusion simply reflects the volatility of the commodity market itself.

Because of this volatile condition, it has been necessary to set limits as to how much any given commodity is allowed to fluctuate in price during any trading day. There is a prescribed unit of fluctuation for each. It is called a point, which, as you remember, on the stock market is $1.00. On the commodity market a point is usually a fraction of 1¢—in the grains, it is ⅛ of 1¢. This means that if you own a job lot, or 1000 bushels, of rye, for example, and the price goes up ⅛ of 1¢ per bushel, you make $1.25. If it goes up one whole cent, you make $10.

When you open a commodity account, the broker doesn't ask if it is to be cash or margin, because there is only one kind —margin, which means, as it does with stocks, that you put down only a percentage of the cost of the contract you are trading. You can open a commodity account with your $1000 and usually with less in Canada, whereas to buy or sell stocks on margin you would have to have at least $2000. Each firm sets its own commodity margin requirements, and they are relatively low—often 10%.

With commodities, you trade in contracts to deliver (if you sell) or to take delivery (if you buy). Each commodity has several regular delivery months in the future, which is why commodity contracts are called futures. A contract is for a specified number of units, which varies with the commodity: a contract of eggs, for example, is 18,000 dozen; of cottonseed oil, 60,000 pounds; of any kind of unprocessed grain, 5000 bushels. The job lot of 1000 bushels of grain is, as has been said, available only in Canada—there are no job lots in anything else.

Commodities are always used by somebody eventually, but no trader expects to make or take delivery of the commodity he sells or buys. He will always make an off-setting purchase or sale before the delivery date—at a profit, he hopes, or a loss, if he has to. In any case, he will never take possession of even 1000 bushels of grain—or deliver them.

If you are "long" a commodity contract, you own it; if you are "short," you have sold it when you didn't own it. In the commodity market, short selling is routine and often advisable, even for the beginner. You can sell short at any time, but of course you know that sooner or later you will have to buy a contract that will offset, or liquidate, the one sold—all shorts have to cover sometime. That's the law, and there is an old rhyme that makes it easy to remember:

> He who sells what isn't his'n
> Must buy it back or go to prison.

A number of American firms are members of the Winnipeg Grain Exchange, but their minimum account and margin requirements are usually higher than those of Canadian firms. Occasionally, you will find a small outfit in the States whose margin, commissions, and minimum account requirements are more in line with those in Canada. To locate a broker you can deal with, write to the Secretary, Winnipeg Grain Exchange, 678 Grain Exchange Building, Winnipeg, Manitoba, Canada, and ask for a list of member firms. If you live in the United States, you might ask for the names of any small brokerage houses that have joined the Exchange since the last printed list.

The ideal is to know your broker personally, but you can trade satisfactorily if you don't. You may have to conduct all your business by mail or phone or telegraph, but this isn't a great drawback, because there is little a broker can tell you face to face that he can't at a distance. Practically all commodity brokers send out regular market letters, and these include about all they have to offer in the way of facts and advice.

If you can't see a broker personally, he will send you the necessary forms and you can open an account by mail. Occasionally, a firm won't demand a minimum account, but you will have to have money on deposit with him in order to trade, so it would be wise to have enough to cover several transactions. The firm's membership in the Exchange is your protection.

There are the same two approaches to trading in commodities that there are in stocks: the fundamental and the technical. You should be familiar with both.

The fundamentalist knows that all commodity prices are influenced chiefly by supply and demand. You will be trading in one of the five grains already mentioned, so you will want to know the growing areas for the one you decide on. What is the total average production per year? What is the grain used for? How much is used domestically? How much is exported—and to what countries?

Every commodity follows certain seasonal price patterns. The grains usually go down in price during harvests: the supply is more likely to satisfy demand at this time than at any other. Whatever the season, the supply depends on the size of the most recent crop and on how much may be held over from the previous year.

If an important percentage of the crop is exported, what

happens in other countries will have a bearing on the price. If there is a crop failure in another country using the grain, there will be a greater demand for the Canadian product, and the price will go up. An outbreak of war in such a country usually means a rise in prices, because production there may be curtailed.

Of course, weather is always important where grain is concerned. Weather in areas of the world that grow crops exported from Canada will be reflected in the Winnipeg prices.

For the fundamentalist, general business conditions are primary indicators: if they are good, commodity prices usually go up; if bad, they go down. You might subscribe to a Canadian newspaper and watch changes in unemployment, industrial production, construction, and retail sales—all indicators of business conditions. Such a newspaper might give you more about what happens on the Winnipeg Exchange, although *The Wall Street Journal* publishes the essential figures every day.

You should keep an eye on the price trend of the grain you are interested in. Is the price level up or down from last year at the same time? Is it rising or falling? Whatever is happening, try to find the reason.

Is your grain following its normal seasonal pattern? If prices have been moving in the opposite direction, the reason will be important.

You will want to know what demand prospects are. Are they better or worse than last year? If your grain is used for feed, check the livestock supply. If it is a raw material for an industry (rye for liquor, for example), how is that industry doing and what are its demands for raw material going to be?

If your grain is exported, you will want to check on foreign production. How does it compare with a year ago? What are its prospects for the current year? Some of the biggest price jumps in Canadian grain have come when there were crop failures abroad.

Keep your eye on competitive products. Oats, for example, are directly competitive with corn. Both are used in feed mixes by ranchers and feed lot operators. The 1970 corn crop in the

United States was so large that it drove prices down; as a result there might be some importation into Canada and this would have a depressing effect on oat prices there. Remember that in commodities you trade short as well as long, so declining prices are just as important as those that rise.

The fundamentalist believes that news influences prices, that some events develop over a period of time, and that if you see this happening soon enough it is sometimes possible to take a position in the market that will let you profit on the outcome. Currency devaluation is an example. The devaluation of the American dollar means that importers in the United States will have to pay more for what they bring in from Canada—rye and oats usually—and this tends to push their prices up.

The technical approach to commodity trading relies on charts, and the chartist maintains that you can't get really accurate figures on supply and demand. Such figures, he says, can be reliable only as they apply to the past; if they have anything to do with the future, they are only guesses—and people have a tendency to guess the way they'd like things to be rather than the way they will be—which no one can tell anyhow.

The chartist's attitude toward news is that it leaks out rather than appears all at once; therefore, a lot of people hear it before it becomes generally known and its principal effect has taken place before it is published. The chartist says also that nobody can interpret news accurately, and he can give you endless examples of people interpreting the same news in different ways as far as its probable effect on trading is concerned.

The chartist admits that traders who act on the fundamentalist guidelines do affect prices, but he says what you really need to know is what the prices are doing, not why. He can show evidence that traders don't always react rationally anyway. If their general mood is good, some highly placed official can make some public prophecy of trouble ahead and the traders will be so preoccupied with their optimism that they'll hardly notice it—and sometimes, when everybody is in a bearish state of mind, it doesn't change things a bit to have word come from on high that everything is going to be just fine. This being so, charts are a truer indicator of how things will be going than any statistics or news.

There is a great deal to be said for both points of view, and you should include both in any decisions you make about commodities. Charts and their interpretation are a long subject and too complicated to deal with here. Some brokerage houses publish booklets explaining them, and there are books. The Commodity Research Bureau, 140 Broadway, New York, New York 10005, has a weekly chart service that covers the grains traded in Winnipeg. If you write them, they'll give you details and prices.

Or you can make a very useful chart yourself and keep it current with not more than five minutes' work a day. It will be one of the variety called the daily high-low-close bar chart. Get a sheet of graph paper; along the vertical edges put the prices in the normal range of the grain you are interested in and along the bottom the dates, leaving out Saturdays, Sundays, and holidays. Each day, draw a vertical line from the low price to the high, with a small cross line at the closing price. You can use as a model the chart of the Dow Jones Averages, published every day on the inside of the back page of *The Wall Street Journal*.

This kind of chart is worth keeping, because it will show price trends, and trends are where you make the real money in commodities. And at this point we come to a major difference between commodity trading and investing in the stock market. With stocks, you handicap yourself if you follow the crowd. In commodities, following the crowd is the only way you can make enough money to justify the effort.

When you begin to trade in commodity futures, you will hear about spreads, straddles, and switches, but until you become a veteran you will be better off in a simple long or short position. (*Position* means you have bought or sold a contract but haven't yet made an offsetting sale or purchase. When you sell what you have bought, or bought to cover what you have sold, you have liquidated your position.) You *buy*, or *go long*,

Chap. 1: a $1000 can be Important & Money

Risk
- to see risks
- measure risk
- know your reactions

Leverage
- 5% leverage

Chap. 2: How To Be a Landlord on $1000

Cheap Buildings
- on leverage
- 3% growth industry
- can profitably sell

Inspection
- is it a hole
  (How to Hire an inspector)

Refinancing
- a loan is not income...
- 2 ways of getting below purchase price

Syndicates
- limited or big
- cost involved
- penalty involved

Chap. 3: How to Invest in Real Estate Without Buying Property

2nd Mortgages
- Discounting

REIT
- a low yield - beware
- sometimes subsidized by banks, etc.
- Magic, June 98%
- 4 profits
- Tax structure very nice
- Wall St. Journal
- Sources:
- Standard & Poor's Stock Reports

Chap. 4: How to Think Like a Sophisticated Investor

Research/how to research
- of young but hungry
- (a) large firm
- good research dept.

Chap. 5: Chiefly for the Bargain Hunter.

Solid Stocks
- utilities
- preferred

Bargains
- 1 dividend
- 2 dividend increase over 10 years
- 3 earnings increase
- 4 price/earning ratio 15 or under
- 5 working capital = price of stock
- 6 Standard & Poor's Stock Reports
- 7 .5 dividend

Current Ratio = assets : liabilities
- 2:1 = good

assets (hidden pitfalls)
- cash
- securities
- receivables
- inventories

How To Make $1000 Grow

Herbert Dalmas

Doubleday & Co, Garden City, New York © 1973

9/11/73

obviously, when you expect the price to go up, so you can sell at a profit. You *sell,* or *go short,* when you expect the price to fall so you can buy an equal amount and profit by the difference.

You never invest in commodities, because you don't keep what you buy for more than a comparatively short time; you trade. Trading in stocks is influenced by the size of brokerage commissions, but those in commodity trading are lower and not such a factor. Trading means buying and selling, and if you are inexperienced, you are likely to be reluctant to take a short position—for example, to sell a contract for 1000 bushels of barley you don't own. But you have to be prepared to do that if it looks as if barley futures were at the beginning of a downward trend. Commodity prices vary so much that if you just stick to buying (long positions) you miss half your opportunities.

Also, all commodity contracts are traded on margin, and you should understand what that means.

If you are trading on 10% margin and go long a contract of grain worth $1000, you only have to put down $100. It is practically unheard of that you—or any other trader—will actually take possession of the grain, so the balance of what the contract is worth, $900, isn't involved.

Now suppose the price of the grain went down 10¢ a bushel. We have seen that a 1¢ change in price means your 10% equity in the contract changes by $10, and now the actual contract is worth only $900. If the price stayed that way until the delivery date, the original contract would have to be paid for. That would mean $1000. If you could sell it, you would only get $900, so you would have lost $100.

If this should happen, you might be miles away, and the broker would have to put up the $900 for you. His job is complicated enough without having to recover involuntary loans.

So when you open an account it is understood that if your equity in a contract goes down 25% you must deposit enough money to bring it back to what it was to begin with. The broker's notification to you that this is necessary is a *margin*

call. You agree that if you don't meet it the broker will liquidate the contract and debit your account 25%.

If the price goes down further, you may get another margin call, and you will know you are on the wrong kind of trend.
The wisest course is never to let the price get to the level where
you will have to put up more margin. When you take a position, give your broker an order to liquidate the contract if it
goes 1¢ against you. This is called a *stop-loss order* and with
it you will never be tempted to stay with your position on the
chance that the price will come back—which is practically
sure ruin in commodity trading. You can take a half dozen 1¢
losses and make them all up, and more, with just one upward
trend.

Before you take a position in a commodity, you should be
familiar enough with supply and demand facts and with charts
to make a guess as to how far up or down the price will go.
You have arranged to stop your loss at 1¢. The potential rise
ought to be at least five times that. You can always liquidate
your position if the rise isn't what the figures have led you to
believe, but you should never take a position expecting to close
out on a small profit. It may seem like an unimportant point,
but it isn't. If you get into the habit of taking small, quick profits, they won't do more than balance your losses, if that. One
thing you must be prepared for in commodities: that is to lose
sometimes. But if you are right 50% of the time and let your
profits run, you will make money.

The chief advantage to a beginner in trading on the Winnipeg Exchange is that it is the only place you can deal in job
lots—1000 bushels. This means smaller margin—and commissions. You won't make a fortune at $10 every time the price
goes with you 1¢, but you won't lose much either if you remember the stop-loss orders—and you will have time to learn. Every
trader has to develop his own techniques and once you have
got yours worked out you can expand your operation—and
your profits.

MUTUAL FUNDS

What mutual funds are and how they operate

Until now, this book has dealt, except in the case of real estate investment trusts, with what you can do with $1000 if you initiate the action and supervise every stage of it from then on. There are many people, however, who have neither the temperament nor the time to do this but who would still like to have some of the benefits of investing. They don't want to "manage" their money—put it into something, realize a profit, then put it into something else; they prefer to have someone else do that for them. These people are usually interested in a continuing program of investing. If they have a great deal of money, they entrust it to an investment counselor, who buys and sells securities to achieve whatever the individual client's objective may be. Such counselors usually don't handle portfolios of less than $25,000, so people with limited amounts to invest get pretty much the same service by putting their money into a mutual fund.

You may decide to put your $1000 into a fund and after that to devote to it only the attention required to read the reports, or you may make it the beginning of a habit. One pleasant thing about a fund is that you can put small amounts into it at any time (usually there is a $25 minimum) and get your full money's worth of shares: it is just as easy to buy 2.326 shares, for example, as it is to buy 2.

The law and their own charters restrict the investment activities of mutual funds: most of them do not lend money, buy on margin, sell short, or deal in real estate or commodities. There are a few funds, however, that are set up specifically to do some of these things—in other words, to speculate, and the best advice about them is to stay away. Speculation is an intensely personal activity. If you go into it, you should make a thorough study of the project you choose; then you should be prepared to devote a lot of time to it, to stay with it, and to act entirely on your own judgment. To let anybody else speculate for you is foolish.

As of the end of 1970, there were more than 800 mutual funds with shares registered for sale in the United States. More than 90% of these are open-end companies, and the others are closed-end. The term "open-end" refers to the buying and selling of shares: there is practically no limit to the number of shares an open-end company can sell, and the buying end is equally open: the company will buy back, or redeem, shares whenever a shareholder asks to have it done.

A closed-end company won't buy back its shares and at the selling end will make an initial offering to the public of a limited number just the way any corporation offers stock. The result is that if you want to buy shares in a closed-end company you have to find someone who already has them, and to sell you need a buyer. The trading process isn't difficult: closed-end companies are listed on the big exchanges or traded over-the-counter, but the price per share on the market is determined by what the buyer or seller thinks it may be worth in the future rather than what its worth actually is at the moment. The real value of any mutual fund share is determined by computing the total value of all its assets at the close of business on any given day and dividing that by the number of shares outstanding. This is called the *net asset value* or *net asset value per share* and is what an investor in an open-end fund pays to join or, when he already owns shares, receives if they are redeemed. In a closed-end fund, the price you pay to join or what you get when you sell is not necessarily the net asset value. It can be more or less, depending on what the people in the market place think about it at the time.

A mutual fund is a corporation with officers and directors who are responsible to the shareholders for what happens to their money. Whereas other corporations, when they list their assets, may include land or buildings or equipment, a mutual fund's assets are only the securities the shareholders' money is invested in, plus a cash reserve all funds maintain to take advantage of market opportunities, to pay expenses, and to redeem shares. The officers and directors formulate and guide the fund's investment policy, but they rarely do the actual investing. For this, they hire an investment management company. The usual fee for management service is about ½ of 1% of the fund's assets per year. Where the management company has done an especially good job, a fund will sometimes add something extra. The other chief expense is brokerage fees paid out for the buying and selling of securities by the management company. These sums are paid before the shareholders get any dividends or capital gains distributions.

These payouts are relatively painless to the shareholders, but there is a charge for joining most funds (called the loading charge), which is impossible to ignore, because it comes out of the amount you invest. It is usually 8½%, though it can go as high as 9%. At 8½%, $85 would come out of your $1000 right away, and that would leave just $915 to be invested. Understandably, people often wonder if they get their money's worth for that 8½%.

For years, there was a saying on Wall Street: "Mutual funds are sold, not bought." When they first appeared on the scene, funds were a complete mystery to most people. Somebody had to go out and tell prospective buyers all about them, and naturally this was a sales job. A mutual fund offers conveniences not so readily available in other kinds of investments. The shareholder can arrange to have his dividends and capital gains distributions automatically applied to the purchase of more shares in the fund. Every cent is used, so that you often get the fractional shares mentioned earlier. The fund's custodial agent handles this kind of thing and keeps all records and sees that you get necessary information when the time comes to fill out your income tax form. The investor doesn't have to bother with stock certificates, and he or she can redeem shares as easily as buy them—simply by sending a written request to the custodian.

Explaining such things was the easiest part of the salesman's job in the early days of the funds. Many people new to the market and without much money to put into it were reluctant to hand their savings over to be managed by someone else. The salesman had to explain the details of how the fund operated and who the people were who would handle the money. And after the sale was made and something went wrong, like a drastic drop in the market that caused the investor to be uneasy or indecisive about whether to stay in or sell out, the salesman was available for support and counsel. He earned the sales charge.

Mutual funds began in this country about 1924, but they didn't start their rapid growth until the 1940s. In 1970 the total assets of all funds was above $54 billion, and in spite of the fact that the SEC won't let them advertise the way insurance companies, for example, do they have become very well known. During the past decade there has been less and less for the salesman to do. People have learned so much about funds and a good deal of the time have liked what they learned that the old saying no longer applied: mutual funds were being bought, and all the salesmen had to do was answer a few questions at the beginning. They got out of the habit of shoring up an investor's morale during bad times.

And there were bad times. In May and June of 1971 the funds were shocked by the fact that they had to pay out more in redemptions than they took in in sales. People had always redeemed their shares for one reason or another, but this was the first time more money had gone out of the funds than had gone in.

A long time ago there were a few funds that didn't levy a sales charge. They were by-products of investment counseling: counseling firms set them up to accommodate the small accounts of the relatives and employees of favored clients. These were pooled together and given the same treatment as the $50,000 and higher portfolios. Nobody paid much attention to them for a long time, but the investment counselors found them profitable. Fifty accounts of $1000 each, lumped together, can be handled as easily as one $50,000 account.

Inevitably, someone got the idea that a mutual fund set up just as all the others had been, only with no sales charge, might have a special appeal. At first, in the "Mutual funds are sold, not bought" days, they didn't do very well, but as mutual funds became better known and more popular and the salesmen didn't seem to be so important, a lot of people began to wonder if the sales charge was worth it. The *no-load funds,* as they came to be called, gave exactly the same service as the others, the same quality of professional management—and more of the investor's money went directly into securities.

So the no-loads grew. In May and June 1971, when the load funds suffered net redemptions for the first time in history, the no-loads took in more in sales than they paid out in redemptions. One no-load took in $34 million more than it paid out as compared with the hardest-hit load fund, which paid out $20 million more than it took in.

The moral of this tale is that if you are looking for a mutual fund to put your $1000 into, either as a one-shot or as the beginning of a continuing program, you ought to include no-loads in your search. Don't base your choice entirely on the presence or absence of the sales charge. A well-run load fund can make enough money for you so that you'll forget all about that 8½% —or it may be so badly managed that you lose money and the $85 bite becomes added injury. If a no-load fund loses you money, you're not going to find much consolation in the fact that you didn't have to pay a sales charge. However, there are no-load funds that have just as efficient management as any with a loading charge—and the $85 will buy several extra shares.

9

How to choose a mutual fund

The first step in choosing a fund is to decide what aspect of investing interests you most: do you want capital appreciation, income, or as much as you can get of both in a combination fund? Do you want as much income as you can get with maximum safety of your capital? Are you interested in putting your money into some special industry? If your $1000 is to be a one-shot investment, probably you should look for growth, the industry's name for capital appreciation. If you are going to have a continuing program, your objective will depend on how old you are, what your income is now and what you expect it to be, and what your present and expected family situations are.

You can find a fund for almost any situation. The majority of funds aim for growth, fewer for income alone, and some try the best combination possible. There are all kinds of variations—funds that invest in the securities of companies in one industry, funds that buy only stocks oriented to science, technology, housing, or whatever; certain funds buy only bonds.

Since one way people rate funds is by performance, it had to happen that there would be funds that made a point of performing as spectacularly as possible. For a while they lighted up the investment sky; they were known as the Go-Go funds and their managers were called gun-slingers—a little enviously sometimes, you suspected, by brokers and managers who were bound to more conservative policies. They stated as their objective maximum capital gain, and most of them used any legitimate means to make as much money as possible in the shortest possible time: they sold short, they bought on margin, they borrowed money. They speculated. And their net asset values soared like broomstick riders on a witches' sabbath.

They had millions to play with and they could see stocks go up or down when they traded fifty or sixty thousand shares, and when the market turned bad toward the end of 1969 they couldn't believe the signs were meant for them. More than 90% of such funds suffered capital losses, some to the verge of disaster.

The point is that a fund, like any other corporation, is people. A fund rises or falls, lives or dies by its management, so before you decide on one, you should know something about the people who manage it. We'll come to that in a moment.

Once you have settled on your objective, you want to find funds that match it. It is logical to limit your search to those that have the best records; there are many ratings of funds, but the most illuminating, when you take everything into account, is the one published by *Forbes* magazine every August. *Forbes* compares each fund's performance with the Standard & Poor's Stock Average, which for this purpose is better than the Dow Jones, because it is based on 500 stocks as compared to the Dow Jones 30. This is an important point, because *Forbes* includes what a fund does in up markets and down markets: a fund will have 100 or more stocks in its portfolio so it will be a fairly sensitive reflection of market behavior in general, and the S&P Average, with its 500 stocks, will reflect market movements in much the same way. *Forbes* lists funds only by name, so the thing to do is make a note of perhaps the best

[86]

dozen or so and then narrow the field further to those whose objectives are your objectives. Incidentally, if your library doesn't have back numbers of *Forbes,* you may have to write them for the most recent August 15 issue. The address is 60 Fifth Avenue, New York, New York 10011.

There are several places you can find fund objectives. One of the most useful is a volume called *Investment Companies,* published each year by Wiesenberger Financial Services. The reference departments of most libraries have this, and you can look at it in many brokerage offices. It is a fine source of data: it has the addresses of funds and a number of useful articles about funds in general. If this book isn't available, ask your bookstore to order the latest *Manual of Mutual Funds* compiled every year by Yale Hirsh, and distributed by Enterprise Press, 527 Madison Avenue, New York, New York 10022. It contains all pertinent data on 500 funds, including addresses, but no ratings.

After you have found six or so funds you feel you might live with compatibly, you will make your final choice. To do this, you'll have to read their prospectuses and that is why you need the fund addresses—so you can send away for them. You might inquire at a brokerage office, and you might find the prospectuses you want. You just might, because a firm usually sells shares in mutual funds—but not in *all* mutual funds, and the prospectuses in any office will be only those of the funds the firm is handling. If the ones you want don't happen to be among them, you are likely to get a pretty strong pitch for the ones they have, so unless you are prepared to resist that, you'd better take the slower course and send away for what you want. Choosing a fund, like choosing any course you take with your money, is your responsibility after all, and you can't be sure you and a fund are meant for each other until you have read the prospectus.

The Securities and Exchange Commission, in its zeal to protect the investing public against intentional or inadvertent hanky-panky by corporations offering stock, has decreed that before any of the stock can be offered for sale full disclosure has to be made about it and the company offering it. This disclosure has to be made in a prospectus, and after the prospectus is published and until the stock is issued and on the market— usually about thirty days—no advertisements can be published with intent to sell. This is called the period of registration.

An open-end mutual fund—load or no-load—is *always* offering stock to the public—all day long, every business day. Therefore the SEC considers a fund to be perpetually in registration, and it may not advertise beyond the stark announcement of its name, its investment objective, and anything special about the kind of fund it is. It may include the suggestion that you send for a prospectus. That is the only way you can find out what you have to know about it: pertinent facts, that is, without any sales talk.

This is all right if you understand in advance that you may be startled, certainly puzzled, and sometimes befuddled in the course of getting to the heart of the matter.

Right on the first page of every prospectus you will find this in heavy upper-case type:

THESE SECURITIES HAVE NOT BEEN APPROVED OR DISAPPROVED BY THE SECURITIES AND EXCHANGE COMMISSION NOR HAS THE COMMISSION PASSED UPON THE ACCURACY OR ADEQUACY OF THIS PRO- SPECTUS. ANY REPRESENTATION TO THE CONTRARY IS A CRIMINAL OFFENSE.

People have found this statement indefinably disquieting, but don't you give it a thought. All it means is, if you think the company is lying or if its stock sinks without a trace, don't come to the SEC with your problem. This is fair enough: there are thousands of corporations in the country and the Commission can't possibly undertake to check the accuracy of every statement made by every one.

You may wonder why the prospectus says something any intelligent person could be expected to take for granted. Like this: "The primary investment objective of the Fund is capital appreciation. There can be no assurance that this objective can be achieved." Obviously—there is risk in all investing. But all fund prospectuses say something like that, and the purpose

[88]

is simply to make it clear that no promises are being made that can't be kept.

All prospectuses give a list of things the Fund is not allowed to do "without shareholder approval." The truth is that in practice the approval or disapproval of mutual fund shareholders is largely theoretical. Owning stock in a fund doesn't really give you the voice you get with stock in other kinds of companies. If you own 10 shares of General Motors, you may go to the annual stockholders' meeting and you can stand up and tell the president how you think the company ought to be run. The odds on anything being done about it won't be very good, but you can be heard, and there is always the chance that what you say may catch the imagination of someone with more influence.

There are mutual fund shareholder meetings, but they are attended almost exclusively by the officers and directors of the Fund. Other shareholders get proxy forms to fill out when there are officers or directors to be elected, but the shareholders themselves don't get together, and the mechanics of their doing anything about how the Fund is managed are so unwieldy that individuals who want to make themselves felt are usually reduced to court action.

The point of mentioning any of this is that, though you should read the prospectus of any fund you are interested in, much of the prose you have to cope with doesn't mean much, and some of it is almost incomprehensible. For example, the following, quoted without additions, changes, or omissions: "The Fund will not: Sell or contract to sell any security which it does not own unless by virtue of its ownership of other securities it has at the time of sale a right to obtain securities without payment of further consideration equivalent in kind and amount to the securities sold and provided that if such right is conditional the sale is made upon the same condition."

After you have spent a few minutes trying to figure that out, you begin to yearn for the cool, still figures of a financial statement. But with funds you are likely to be in as much trouble there unless you are an accountant. You may not be able to find among the numbers certain items you are interested in—brokerage commissions, for example.

The answer is: don't squander a moment on anything in a prospectus that you can't understand instantly. Most of what you really need to know is stated clearly somewhere in the prose: who runs the Fund, who gets the management fee, who the brokers are through whom the Fund managers buy and sell securities, and how much they collect in commissions.

It is the responsibility of the Fund directors to formulate investment policy and to appoint a management company to carry it out. It is not unusual for directors of the Fund to be officers and shareholders of the management company, and there is nothing to be apprehensive about in this: it is logical that people who have the talents to make investment policy would also have the brains to carry it out. What has occasionally raised an eyebrow or so is that sometimes the directors of the Fund who are also part of the management company are also members of the brokerage firms that get the commissions for buying and selling the Fund's securities.

Affiliations like this have been known to create a temptation to churn an account, which is the old Wall Street expression for excessive trading with the commissions first in mind and the good of the portfolio second. The fact that the temptation exists doesn't mean that it is succumbed to; the point is that there is no way of knowing unless the prospectus tells you specifically. Financial statements merely show the total assets at the end of stated periods; they say nothing about how often or why management has been in and out of the market between times. If commissions are high and the capital gains distributions low, shareholders sometimes feel that they should have had some of the money that went to the brokers—and this is the kind of thing that can cause court action.

The prospectus will tell you how you can buy shares, exactly what the sales charge is, and how you go about redeeming shares. If there is a minimum investment to open your account, the prospectus will tell you, and it will tell you the minumum for subsequent share purchases. These are things you have to know.

There will be information on the automatic reinvestment of dividends and capital gains distributions, which is one of the mutual funds' most attractive features. You usually can have either or both reinvested automatically even if they don't pay for the minimum you would have to buy if you bought with cash. And even the load funds don't levy a sales charge for this service.

Most funds have a withdrawal plan by which you can arrange to have a set sum paid to you every month or every three months. This won't be immediately interesting to you with $1000 to invest, because there is a required minimum of $10,000, but if you decide to make a regular program of fund investing you should know that it's possible.

How can you calculate the probability that the fund you choose will make money for you? Your impulse may be to look at the figures near the front of the prospectus under the heading "Statement of Per Share Income and Capital Changes." This shows, among other things, dividends and capital gains distributions, which is the money the Fund pays you every year, and the net asset value, which is what you pay to buy into the Fund or what you get when you redeem shares. Remember that this figure in the statement is approximate for the time you are reading it, because the net asset value per share is always changing.

These figures are for at least the past ten years (or for the life of the fund if it hasn't existed that long). Naturally, you'd like dividends and capital gains distributions to show an unbroken upward trend, but that isn't likely because of the built-in sensitivity of a fund's portfolio to general market movements, so those figures will be down in the bad years.

At this point you should go back to the *Forbes* ratings. Each fund is rated according to its performance in three rising markets and three declining markets, and the rating is in relation to other funds. A+ means the top 12½%; A is the next 12½%, B is the next 25%, and so on. *Forbes* doesn't include this item for new funds, because they haven't had time to work through three rising and three falling markets; however, of 162 established load funds rated in the August 15, 1971 issue, only 4 got ratings of B or better in both rising and falling markets. Thirty-seven no-load funds were rated, and of those 4 did B or better up and down.

Of course, if you foresee a rising market, you may want to get into a fund with a high rating on that side even if it is lower for the bear markets. Here there may be an advantage in a no-load, other factors being equal. Although some charge a redemption fee (the prospectuses will tell you), the absence of the sales charge will make it easier to get out if the market stops going up—you are less likely to feel the commitment you do where you have had to give up 8½% of your initial investment.

10

What the critics say

Critics of funds have a number of favorite objections; some of them are still valid, and others have lost some of the merit they may have had at one time.

It is often said that funds are too big, that their vast resources make it possible for them to jolt the market with their 50,000- or 60,000-share transactions in a way that is harmful even to the average investor. It is true that funds still have great impact, but it is unfair to suggest that they are alone in this. There are other institutional investors who swing just as much weight in the market, and the funds' assets are hardly impressive compared to what the insurance companies have.

Second, there is the sales charge, but that criticism is losing force as the no-loads increase and the public learns more about them. More and more, the emphasis is on what the funds do rather than on what they cost.

Third, critics have maintained that the funds' emphasis on diversification is misleading. If you put your money into a fund, you are not diversifying, because you are investing in only *one* security. It is the company you are investing in that diversifies. The value of your investment goes up or down depending on how good management is, just the way it does, at least in part, in any other company—and a fund doesn't have a good product to compensate for subnormal performance by management.

The primary reason for diversifying is that, when one issue or more in your portfolio goes down, the others don't necessarily follow, and your risk averages less. But the diversification in a fund's portfolio is sometimes so great that its securities practically span the market and, when the market goes down, so many of the fund's securities go with it that the advantages, if any, of diversification are diluted.

Fourth, the critics point out that, in spite of the fact that mutual fund salesmen don't have to do the instructing and hand-holding they used to have to do, there is still a great deal of pressure selling, which sometimes obscures the facts. Even the no-loads channel their buying and selling of securities to brokerage firms that plug their funds—and of course "reciprocal business" has been a fixture with most funds for years. There is nothing unethical about this, but there is no doubt that it tends to work against the small investor. It is no secret that individual brokers don't welcome opening small accounts. If someone comes in with $500 to $5000 to invest, the broker will probably do his best to steer it into a mutual fund. This saves time and gets the broker a satisfactory share of the loading charge, but the fund he suggests will be one his firm handles—and no firm handles them all, or even a large segment of what is available. The contention is that in a situation like this the emphasis is only secondarily, if at all, on seeing that the investor gets matched up with a fund that is really in his best interest.

Another criticism is that the management fee isn't always justified. One half of 1% doesn't sound like much when you say it, and ½ of 1% doesn't look like much when you read it, and in a small fund it is a relatively modest sum: if the total assets are $1 million, it is only $5000.

However, there are many funds with assets over $100 mil-

lion and some with assets of more than $1 billion. One half of
1% of that figure is $5 million, which is a handsome fee for a
year's work, no matter how arduous. The thing is that the managers of a $1 billion fund could maintain very nearly that level
in a normal market with very little effort, and the pay would
be the same $5 million. Even in a fund with assets, say, of $200
million, the figures give you pause. The fee figured on that
would be $1 million, and if the managers were able to increase
the fund's assets by $10 million in one year, their fee would
be calculated on the gain plus the $200 million that was al-
ready there. The critics say that the increase is the gauge of
their performance and that some arrangement should be
worked out so that they aren't paid year after year on the
basis of what they have done in previous years.

Whether the critics have a point here or not, the reality is
that, as far as the individual shareholder is concerned, the
management bite is painless. It is simply money you don't get
and never see, and if what you have in the fund increases by
10% or 12% a year, as it does in many funds, you don't think
about details that, from where you sit, are largely theoretical.

Nobody questions the advantages of professional money
management, but the critics say that it isn't always adequate
compensation to the investor for being locked into a fund. A
fund shareholder shouldn't and hardly ever does simply ignore the market. No matter what security your money is in,
once you are in the market you almost inevitably become interested in it. Every professional manager is not as good as
every other, and none of them is infallible. There may come
a time when you think the managers of your fund are not doing as well as they could—maybe not even as well as you
could yourself.

Critics say the sales charge makes getting in and out of the
market so costly that you are almost never able to do it profitably from a fund. In and out brokerage commissions are
never as great as a mutual fund sales charge. As was pointed
out in the previous chapter, this criticism is met to some extent
by the no-load funds.

Critics have been particularly voluble in their objections to what is called the contractual plan, or front-end load fund. These are not as aggressively promoted as they were a few years ago, but they are still around.

Their best feature was supposed to be that the investor signed a contract to put in so much money every month for ten or twelve years. In this way he was forced to save, which was in his interest—saving is a good habit not enough people get into.

The critics say the front-end loaders play down the fact that one half of what the investor puts in during the first year goes to commissions. The percentage decreases afterward so that the sales charge averages out over the life of the contract to the regular 8½%, but in the beginning the benefit is mostly with the salesman.

This is all right unless the investor wants to cancel the contract and redeem his shares. Usually he can't expect to break even until he has held the contract for about three years unless there has been a pretty big increase in net asset value. If the market goes down, it could be five or six years—or longer. The salesman, however, gets his cut right away, no matter what.

Mutual funds have been called investing with the excitement and fun removed, and by and large this is true. But if you don't have the time or temperament for that kind of pleasure, and if you choose your fund wisely, it can be a satisfactory way to get into the market and a profitable way of staying there.

A FEW
CLOSING OBSERVATIONS

11

Things to remember

Everybody has heard stories like the one about the highboy bought at auction in a Pennsylvania farmhouse for $20 that turned out to be a $30,000 Chippendale, or the old painting in the attic that Aunt Amanda thought looked too fuzzy to hang in the living room and proved to be an original Monet—and some of them are true. But before you try to make money with your $1000 in art or antiques or various other highly special- ized fields, you should keep in mind that the commonplace outnumber the valuable articles by a ratio no one can calcu- late. Learning what you need to know in those fields, if you are to make money in them, is a lot different from learning what you need to know in the financial world or in real es- tate. In those two areas, it is possible to have a pretty clear idea of the scope of what you don't know and therefore of what you must find out in order to make money with money and learning is neither long nor very difficult; but the study of antiques or art, for instance, can be a career. The safest course to follow where they are concerned is to buy what you like because you like it and not for potential capital gain.

The same applies to other specialties like books and coins and stamps. There are treasures to be found, but you aren't likely to find them unless you make a major career of the search. There is a little of the collector in almost everybody, but if you decide to be one, do it for fun or whatever collectors call it—not to make money.

As we have said before, make it a rule not to get into anything financially where adequate information is not readily available. It is just as important not to assume that it isn't available. Anybody who has had experience in Wall Street will warn you against the hot tip. A hot tip occurs when someone tells you that his brother has it straight from a cousin of the president of Fabulous, Inc., that Fabulous is coming out with a washing machine that washes clothes with sound waves, and the stock is bound to go up about 80 points as soon as the news breaks.

This preposterous idea was made the basis of a movie produced by a prominent brokerage house in New York some twenty years ago. The hero was a nice-looking, good-natured idiot, who was saved from the consequences of his folly by his more sensible wife and the firm's research department. Just as the movie was about to be released, somebody discovered that there actually was a washing machine that used sound waves and that the company making it was listed on the New York Stock Exchange and was doing quite well. There was hasty rewriting and numerous retakes.

The point is that there is nothing wrong with a hot tip just because it is a hot tip. True, the odds are that it will lead nowhere, but you can't really be sure, can you, until you look into it? Where the hot tip cools is when it is impossible to get information, but it shouldn't take long to get to where you know that. And you certainly should go that far. A few years ago the proprietor of a store in a small California town told a customer that his brother was working for a firm that was about to be awarded a big government contract and that the stock would be a wise buy because only a very few people knew about the contract.

The customer knew his way around and wasn't about to fall for a tip as blatantly hot as all that. He thanked the storekeeper in an amused manner and went his way. And the company did get the contract and the stock went up steadily for more than a year, and the customer could have found the facts with very little trouble. He didn't because he *assumed* they were impossible to get—he didn't *know*.

Sometimes what you need to know really is impossible to find out. This can happen with the so-called penny stocks. These are mostly the stocks of mining companies, usually in Canada or northwestern United States, whose stocks often sell for less than a dollar. The thought of being able to buy 5000 shares of something for $500 is heady stuff, and a lot of people do it. Some are lucky if the stock just doesn't go anywhere—but sometimes such stocks do go up and the holders make a lot of money.

In such companies there is always a lot to hear about, but the facts you need are exactly the same as with any stock you are considering. If you can't find the pertinent balance sheet figures, recognize the situation for what it is and forget it as a place to put your money. This rule sounds easy, but there is always a temptation to believe what you would like to believe, especially when you think there could be so much money in what you would like to believe.

One of the most important warnings to hang in a prominent place if you are about to put money into a project is to be governed by reason and not by prejudice or your emotions. You may think highly of the shoes you wear, but before you invest in the company that makes them, be sure to check on every point you would check on if you had no interest in the product at all. And if you buy the stock, don't hold onto it from a sense of loyalty if the usual indicators say to sell.

One area where emotion has lost money for a great many people in the United States is real estate in parts of the country where there are sizable stretches of undeveloped land. A promoter will buy several thousand acres of such land for very little per acre. He will then subdivide it into "estates" or "ranchos," depending on where it is, and advertise lavishly that here is the vacation hideaway for you and your family that you have always dreamed about. Sometimes there is a free plane trip to Dreamland, or whatever the name happens to be, with conducted tours showing where everything is going to be when all is complete. The country is beautiful, and if you work in the city, the prospect of having a house in those surroundings has a pretty strong emotional pull. To make it stronger, the terms are a small amount down with easy monthly payments that include everything—taxes and all. Some promotions even throw in, for a small additional charge, a prefab house that you and your family or friends can put up on your land in a couple of fun-filled weekends.

Your land—deep in almost everybody there is something that responds to those words. The emotional appeal is so great that these promotions make money for the promoter. And if you would really like a little house in the wilds, if it is near enough to your home and your work to be practical as a vacation spot, perhaps you should think about buying it.

Before you do, however, reinforce what your emotions say with a bit of thinking. Payments go on for years. They look easy when you start: your $1000 will often cover the down payment, and you can see how you can juggle your budget so the monthly payments won't be a problem. Maybe they never will be, but there is always the unexpected and something could happen that would make it impossible for you to keep them up.

There may have been an implication that you can always sell the land if you decide sometime that you don't want a private vacation paradise—or if you can't continue the payments. Implication or not, the odds are that you won't be able to sell it. Practically all land in these developments is sold by contract, and in a contract sale of real estate the title stays with the seller until the entire purchase price has been paid. If the buyer defaults on a payment or two he loses all claim to the property and often all the money he has put into it. And even if you have made all the payments and want to sell, remember you won't have the promoter's sales force, and if you try to sell before he has got rid of all the ranchos in the development you will be competing with his salesmen.

Another rule is that you make money with money only in practice, never in theory. An institution like the stock market is likely to inspire a certain amount of awe in the uninitiated because of the publicity it gets, and even if you have the capacity to do the work necessary to make money there and the temperament to handle your investments after you make them, you may find it hard to take the first step.

If you have this hesitancy, there is the temptation to persuade yourself that you ought to do a little practicing first. You do all the preliminary work just as if you were going to buy the security, but instead of committing money to it, you make your investment on paper, then see how you would have done if you had actually put your money into the market.

You can learn that way, but not enough. If you take a theoretical loss (or gain) on a theoretical investment, you have no real incentive to try to find out why, and unless you know the reason for what you did wrong, it's difficult to guard against doing it again, and if you don't know why you were right, it's hard to repeat.

One way to get over this is to get someone else to join you in taking the plunge. In real estate, there is the small syndicate that will do it; in the stock market, you can form an investment club.

An investment club is a group of people, usually not less than twelve or more than twenty—all men, all women, or mixed. The vital considerations are that they get along together, that their financial situations are pretty much the same, and that they have the same point of view toward committing their money. No decisions would ever be made if half the club were conservative and the other half swingers.

An investment club gives you the moral support that comes from sharing an experience with people whose level of knowledge is about the same as your own. You have regular meetings at which you can talk over what you plan to do and what you have done. If an investment has made money, you can help one another analyze why; if there has been a paper loss, there are other ideas than your own as to what went wrong and what to do about it. This actually works out: statistics show that in the third to fifth year of a club's operation almost every member will open an account of his or her own—while maintaining membership in the club.

If you organize a club and the decision is to have each member contribute $10 a month, your $1000 will guarantee participation for eight years. (Of course you would put the money into a savings account so the part that didn't go into the club would be drawing interest.) If the monthly contribution were $20, you would be good for four years without exceeding the $1000.

In many ways, an investment club is like a miniature mutual fund. A club must have a legal entity so that it can have a brokerage account and so that some individual can be empowered to act with the broker in the club's name. A club can be a corporation but that involves fees you don't really have to pay; a formal partnership will do just as well.

One big difference between a club and a mutual fund is that buying into a fund is simple, while joining a club after it has been formed is expensive and complicated. The essence of the club concept is that each member contribute and share exactly as every other member does. If you join a club that has been going for three years, each member paying $10 a month, you would have to pay $360 just to equal what the other members have contributed. If the club's portfolio has increased in value, it would require some complicated accounting to figure out what your share would be, because neither your money nor your ideas had helped produce the profits. On the whole, it is best for the members to start together and stay together with no additions. Unless, of course, there is an accountant in the club.

It is helpful to have a lawyer in the group to see that all legal requirements are met, but that isn't absolutely necessary. The club will, however, have to deal with a broker and the broker can't be a member. Most brokerage firms prohibit this and they even prefer that no registered representative assist in the formation of a club. But there will have to be one to handle the account and he should be chosen early. When the club is ready to discuss its first investment, he should be at the meeting. Investment clubs are so popular that the New York Stock Exchange has drawn up guidelines for the brokers on their accounts. At this first meeting, the NYSE asks that the broker:

1. Explain how the club account will be handled.
2. Explain the services his firm is prepared to render.
3. Explain that the club will be treated by his firm as an individual customer and that, although all investment decisions will be made by the members as a group, one member should be appointed to deal directly with the broker in the club's behalf.

He will stress this last point. It is important that the club should understand that individual members should not call the broker's office to ask about the club's account or about any securities the club may be considering or about prices of securities the club already owns.

According to recent estimates, there are some 60,000 investment clubs in existence. If you want to think about forming one, write to National Association of Investment Clubs, Dept. O, 1515 E. Eleven Mile Road, Royal Oak, Michigan 48067.

Finally, what about advice? There is never any lack of it— you will see advisory services advertised for every field you can put money into.

Advice doesn't include offers to show you, for a small charge, how to make a fortune. If someone offers you a chance to invest in a project, look into it just the way you would into any listed stock and make your decision on the caliber of the people behind it and on what you believe the chances of success to be. But if somebody sends you a letter or advertises in a magazine that for a mere pittance he can show you how to make fabulous sums, ask yourself why he doesn't just do it himself and retire.

You may find that some advisory services are worth the money you pay for them, but you should remember that advice is never better than an informed opinion, and you should never act on it blindly. You should look into it with the same care you'd bring to a company's earnings record and balance sheet and management.

What you really need, first and always, is information. You will always find a good deal in any large metropolitan newspaper. *The Wall Street Journal* is a steady and reliable channel of it, with expert comment added. The *Journal* is published daily except Saturdays, Sundays, and holidays, and there are regional editions. *Barron's* is a weekly, published every Monday, which has the latest earnings information (among other things) about every stock listed on both the big exchanges and many of those traded over-the-counter. *Forbes* is published twice a month and is helpful if you are going into the stock market. *Changing Times* comes out every month; it is subtitled "The Kiplinger Service for Families" and it deals expertly and in plain language with most things concerning money. You may come across others that will seem valuable to you.

The most important thing of all to remember is that whatever the situation, however involved or simple the way you choose to make money with money, the responsibility for all decisions invariably comes back to the same place: yourself.

Index

Price/earnings ratio, 44–45, 46, 49
Prices, commodities, 71
Profit limit, 14
Profits, 3–4, 58, 95; in commodities, 67, 76; in options, 61–62, 63–64; in real estate, 12, 21, 27; in stock investments, 41, 42, 43, 46, 53
Prospectuses, 87, 91
Purchase contract, 18
Puts, 55, 61–65

Real estate, 9–31; contracts, 18–19; defined, 9–10; depreciation allowance, 17; examples, 10–12; financing, 19–21; how to choose a house, 13–16; improvements, 16; second mortgages, 25–27; signing documents, 14; syndicates, 21–24; taxes on, 17–18; trusts, 27–31
Real Estate Investment Trust Act, 27
Real estate investment trusts, 27–31; how to choose, 30
Redemptions, mutual fund, 82, 83, 96; fees, 92
Reference books, 44, 60, 64, 74, 87; real estate, 14, 23
Refinancing, 13, 20
Reinvestment, automatic, 91
REIT. *See* Real estate investment trusts
Rents, 12, 16, 17, 20, 28
Reports, company's annual, 48, 53
Rights, stock, 55–56
Rising market, 36, 37, 52–53, 86, 91–92
Risk, 2, 13, 41–42, 43, 67. *See also* Speculation
RKO warrants, 58
Rothschilds, the, 37
Round lots, 51. *See also* Job lots; Odd lots

Sales charge, 83, 91, 93, 95
Salesmen, 82, 83, 94
Savings accounts, 4
Savings and loan associations, 3, 4, 10, 21, 25, 50
Second mortgage, 11, 18, 25–27
Securities and Exchange Commission, 29, 61, 82, 87–88
Short-term mortgage trusts, 27, 28–29
Short trading, 70, 73, 75
Specialty investments, 99–100
Speculation, 2, 37, 43, 56; and mutual funds, 80, 86; in new firms, 47, 48; and puts and calls, 64–65. *See also* Risk

Speculator, commodity, 68 (defined), 69
Split stocks, 42–43, 59
Standard & Poor's Manual, 60
Standard & Poor's Stock Average, 86
Standard & Poor's Stock Reports, 30, 44–45, 46, 47, 49, 50, 52, 59, 60
Stock market, 35–65; the Average, 37–38; balance sheets, 49–51; bargains, 43–53; best buying time, 52–53; brokers, 38–40; clues to undervalued stock, 45–47; examples, 46–47; general description, 35–65; how to choose a bargain, 44–46; management, 48–49; new companies, 47; optional courses, 41–42, 55; puts and calls, 61–63; rights, 56; technical and fundamental view, 36–37; warrants, 56–61; writing options, 63–65
Stop-loss order, 76
Striking price, 61, 62
Success, rules for, 2
Surcharges, 38
Syndicate, real estate, 21–24

Taxes, 10, 16–17, 82; deductions on real estate, 12, 17–18, 28
Technical view of stock market, 36–37, 71, 73
Temperament and investment climate, 2, 5, 21–22, 79–80
Theoretical investments, 103
Tips, market, 100–1
Title search, 19–20
Tri-continental warrants, 59

Undervalued stock, 41, 43, 44 (defined), 45–46
Undeveloped land, 101–2
Unimproved land, 10
Units, commodity, 70
Utilities, 50

Wall Street Journal, The, 30, 40, 43, 48, 51, 72, 74, 106
Warrants, 55, 56–61, 62; example, 56–57; expiration date, 60; premium, 57
Weisenberger Financial Services, 87
Winnipeg Grain Exchange, Canada, 68, 70, 71 (address), 72, 74, 76
Withdrawal plan, mutual funds, 91

Yield, 43–44